APPROXIMATE JOURNEY TIMES BY ROAD

- GLASGOW 230 mins
- EDINBURGH 230 mins
- NEWCASTLE UPON TYNE 120 mins
- LEEDS 15 mins
- HULL 60 mins
- WAKEFIELD
- LIVERPOOL 60 mins
- BIRMINGHAM 110 mins
- NORWICH 220 mins
- CARDIFF 210 mins
- BRISTOL 180 mins
- LONDON 190 mins
- DOVER 290 mins
- PORTSMOUTH 250 mins

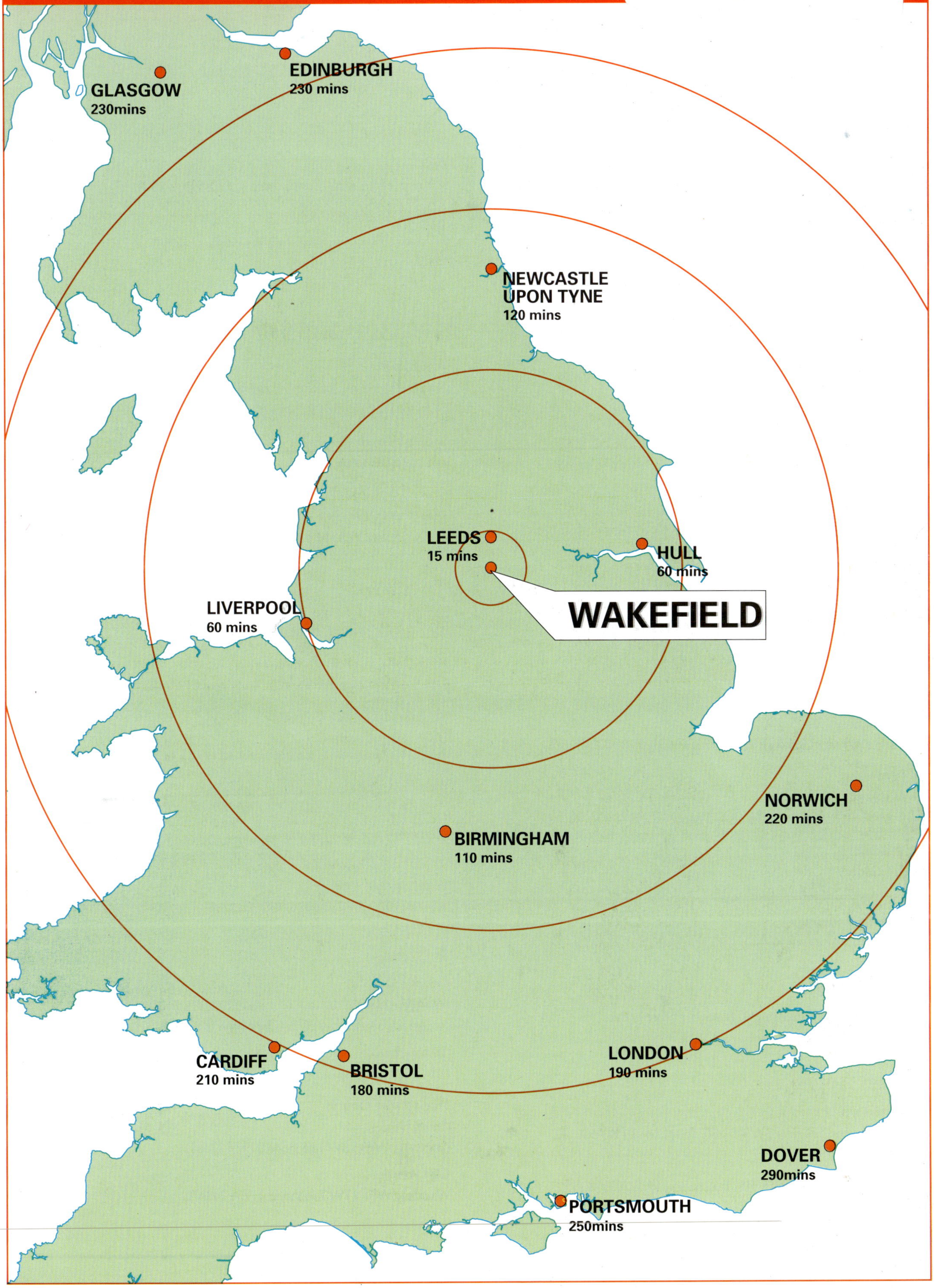

PRINCIPAL TOURIST ATTRACTIONS

Chantry Chapel of St. Mary
Wakefield Bridge, Wakefield. Telephone 01924 373847.

Hemsworth Water Park
Hoyle Mill Road, Kinsley, Hemsworth WF9 5JB. Telephone 01977 617617.

Light Waves Leisure Centre
Marsh Way, Wakefield WF1 3LJ. Telephone 01924 302330.

National Coal Mining Museum for England
New Road, Overton, Nr. Wakefield WF4 4RH. Telephone 01924 848806.

Newmillerdam Country Park
Barnsley Road, Wakefield. Telephone 01924 303980.

Nostell Priory
Nostell, Nr. Wakefield WF4 1QD. Telephone 01924 863892.

Pontefract Castle
Micklegate, Pontefract WF8 1QG. Telephone 01977 600208.

Pugneys Country Park
Asdale Road, Off Denby Dale Road, Wakefield WF2 7EQ. Telephone 01924 302360.

Ridings Shopping Centre
Wakefield WF1 1DS. Telephone 01924 787789.

Sandal Castle
Manygates Lane, Sandal, Wakefield.

Wakefield Cathedral
Cathedral Precinct, Wakefield WF1 1HG. Telephone 01924 373923.

Yorkshire Sculpture Park
West Bretton, Nr. Wakefield WF4 4LG. Telephone 01924 830302.

LOCAL INFORMATION

● ART GALLERIES AND MUSEUMS

Castleford
Museum
Carlton Street, Castleford WF10 1BB. Telephone 01977 722085.

Pontefract
Museum
Salter Row, Pontefract, WF8 1BA. Telephone 01977 722740.

Wakefield
Art Gallery
Wentworth Terrace, Wakefield WF1 3QW. Telephone 01924 305796.

Wakefield Museum
Wood Street, Wakefield WF1 2EW. Telephone 01924 305351.

● BUS SERVICES

West Yorkshire Passenger Transport Executive
40/50 Wellington Street, Leeds LS1 2DE. Telephone 0113 251 7272.

● BUS STATIONS

Castleford
Albion Street, Castleford WF10 1EG. Telephone 01977 552142.

Pontefract
Horsefair, Pontefract WF8 1PE. Telephone 01977 703366.

Wakefield
Bullring, Wakefield WF1 3AG. Telephone 01924 360000.

For **METRO** local bus and train enquiries telephone 0113 245 7676.

● CHAMBER OF COMMERCE AND INDUSTRY

Mid Yorkshire Chamber of Commerce
New Commerce House, 168 Westgate, Wakefield WF2 9SR. Telephone 01924 200646.

● CINEMAS

ABC
Kirkgate, Wakefield WF1 1JG. Telephone 01924 373400.

Cineworld the Movies
Colinsway, Westgate Retail Park, Wakefield. Telephone 01924 332250.

● CITIZEN'S ADVICE BUREAU

Ossett
32 Station Road, Ossett WF5 8AD. Telephone 01924 270177.

Pontefract
1B Charter House, Jacksons Court, Pontefract WF8 1DE. Telephone 01977 793768.

South Elmsall
Westfield Resource & Enterprise Centre, Westfield Lane South Elmsall WF9 2PU. Telephone 01977 642179.

Wakefield
27 King Street, Wakefield WF1 2SR. Telephone 01924 372563.

● COLLEGES

Bretton Hall College
West Bretton, WF4 4LG. Telephone 01924 830261.

New College, (Post 16 Centre)
Park Lane, Pontefract, WF8 4QR. Telephone 01977 702139.

Wakefield District College
Hemsworth Centre
Station Road, Hemsworth WF9 4JL. Telephone 01924 789789.

Wakefield Centre
Margaret Street, Wakefield WF1 2DQ. Telephone 01924 789789.

Whitwood Business Faculty
Four Lane Ends, Whitwood WF10 5NF. Telephone 01924 789789.

Woolley Hall College
Woolley WF4 2JR. Telephone 01226 382509.

● COURTS

County Courts
Horsefair House
Horsefair, Pontefract WF8 1RJ. Telephone 01977 702357.

Crown House
127 Kirkgate, Wakefield WF1 1JW. Telephone 01924 370268.

Magistrates Courts
Court House
Pontefract WF8 1BW. Telephone 01977 723601.

Cliff Parade
Wakefield WF1 2TW. Telephone 01924 303470.

● EARLY CLOSING DAYS

Castleford: Wednesday.

Featherstone: Wednesday.

Ferrybridge: Staggered.

Hemsworth: Staggered.

Horbury: Staggered.

Knottingley: Thursday.

Normanton: Wednesday.

Ossett: Tuesday.

Pontefract: Thursday.

South Elmsall: Wednesday.

South Kirkby: Thursday.

Wakefield: Wednesday (most shops operate six day trading).

● ELECTRICITY

Yorkshire Electricity plc
P.O. Box 161, Gelderd Road, Leeds LS12 6EE. Telephone 0113 241 5000.

Bill Enquiries: Telephone 0113 279 0133.

Emergency Calls: Telephone 01977 553821.

Offer (Office of Electricity Regulation)
Symons House, Belgrave Street, Leeds LS2 8DD.
Telephone 0113 234 1866.

● GAS

Billing Enquiries: Telephone 0645 555600.

Service Calls/Enquiries: Telephone 0645 650650.

Gas Escapes: Freephone 0800 111999.

Gas Consumer Council
North East Office, 1 Eastgate, Leeds LS2 7RL. Telephone 0113 243 9961.

● HEALTH AUTHORITIES

Wakefield Health Authority
White Rose House, West Parade, Wakefield WF1 1LT.
Telephone 01924 814400.

● HOSPITALS

Castleford, Normanton & District Hospital
Lumley Street, Castleford WF10 5LT. Telephone 01977 605500.

Clayton Hospital
Northgate, Wakefield WF1 3JS. Telephone 01924 201688.

Fieldhead Hospital
Wakefield WF1 3SP. Telephone 01924 201688.

Pinderfields and Pontefract NHS Hospital Trust
Telephone 01924 201688 or 01977 600600.

Southmoor Hospital
Hemsworth WF9 4LU. Telephone 01977 465630.

Stanfeld Unit
Aberford Road, Wakefield WF1 4DQ. Telephone 01924 201688.

● INFORMATION CENTRE

Town Hall
Wood Street, Wakefield WF1 2HQ. Telephone 01924 305000/1.

● INLAND REVENUE

HM Inspector of Taxes
4 Horsefair
Pontefract WF8 1PB. Telephone 01977 692700.

Crown House
127 Kirkgate, Wakefield WF1 1JL. Telephone 01924 215400.

Valuation Offices
District Valuer and Valuation, 42 Eastgate, Leeds LS2 7JT. Telephone 0113 228 4500.

● JOB CENTRES/UNEMPLOYMENT BENEFIT OFFICES

Centurian House
Bank Street, Castleford, WF10 1HY. Telephone 01977 463200.

Low Hall
Market Street, Hemsworth WF9 4LF. Telephone 01977 611324.

King Edward Street,
Normanton WF6 2BB. Telephone 01924 220590.

King Charles II House
Pontefract WF8 1DD. Telephone 01977 463100.

Crowther House
Thornhill Street, Wakefield WF1 1PL. Telephone 01924 322100.

● LIBRARIES

Headquarters and Reference Library
Balne Lane, Wakefield WF2 0DQ. Telephone 01924 302210.

Major Libraries
Carlton Street, Castleford WF10 1BB. Telephone 01977 722085.

Shoemarket, Pontefract WF8 1BD. Telephone 01924 727692/3.

Drury Lane, Wakefield WF1 2TD. Telephone 01924 305376.

● MARKET DAYS

Castleford
Monday - Saturday (half-day Wednesday & Secondhand Thursday).

Featherstone
Thursday.

Hemsworth
Tuesday, Friday and Saturday (Secondhand Monday).

Normanton
Tuesday and Saturday.

Ossett
Tuesday and Friday (Craft & Flea Market Tuesday & Friday in Town Hall).

Pontefract
Wednesday and Saturday (Craft Market Wednesday in Town Hall).

South Elmsall
Tuesday, Friday and Saturday.

Wakefield
Monday, Tuesday, Thursday, Friday and Saturday. (Carbootless sale Sunday).

POLICE

West Yorkshire Metropolitan Police Headquarters
Laburnum Road, Wakefield WF1 3QS. Telephone 01924 375222.

Principal Stations
Normanton. Telephone 01924 893331.
Pontefract. Telephone 01977 793611.
Wakefield. Telephone 01924 375831.

RAILWAY INFORMATION

For Passenger Train Service Information Telephone 0345 484950 (Calls answered in strict rotation please wait for a reply).

REGISTRATION OF BIRTHS, DEATHS & MARRIAGES

Pontefract Registration District
Town Hall, Pontefract WF8 1PG. Telephone 01977 727670.

Wakefield Registration District
71 Northgate, Wakefield WF1 3BX. Telephone 01924 361635.

RELATE

6 Cheapside, Wakefield WF1 2SD. Telephone 01924 372494.

SAMARITANS

3 Jacob's Well Lane, Wakefield WF1 3NN. Telephone 01924 377011.

SOCIAL SECURITY

Bridge House
28 Wheldon Road, Castleford WF10 2JG. Telephone 01977 464111.

Low Hall
Market Street, Hemsworth WF9 4LF. Telephone 01977 624000.

Enterprise House
22-26 Horsefair, Pontefract WF8 1RG. Telephone 01977 692800.

Crown House
127 Kirkgate, Wakefield WF1 1ST. Telephone 01924 433600.

THEATRES

Theatre Royal & Opera House
Drury Lane, Wakefield WF1 2TE. Telephone 01924 211311.

Powerhouse 1 Showcase Theatre
Smyth Street, Wakefield WF1 1ED. Telephone 01924 211311.

Wakefield Arts Centre
Thornes Park Centre, Horbury Road, Wakefield WF2 8QZ. Telephone 01924 789815.

TOURIST INFORMATION CENTRE

Town Hall
Wood Street, Wakefield WF1 2HQ. Telephone (01924) 305000/1.

UNEMPLOYMENT BENEFIT OFFICES

(See under 'Job Centres')

VOLUNTARY ACTION WAKEFIELD DISTRICT

11 Upper York Street, Wakefield WF1 3LQ. Telephone 01924 367418.

10-12 Finkle Street, Pontefract WF8 1HE. Telephone 01977 797474.

WAKEFIELD METROPOLITAN DISTRICT COUNCIL

Chief Executive Departmental Headquarters
County Hall, Bond Street, Wakefield WF1 2QW. Telephone 01924 306090.

Community & Social Services Department
8 St John's North, Wakefield WF1 3QA. Telephone 01924 307700.

Education Department
County Hall, Bond Street, Wakefield WF1 2QL. Telephone 01924 306090.

Finance Department H.Q.
P.O. Box 55, Newton Bar, Wakefield WF1 2TT. Telephone 01924 306445.

Housing Department
Civic Centre, Castleford WF10 4AN. Telephone 01977 727012.

Public Services Department
Town Hall, Normanton WF6 2DZ. Telephone 01924 307251.

Regeneration Department
Newton Bar, Leeds Road, Wakefield WF1 2TX. Telephone 01924 306090.

WEST YORKSHIRE PROBATION SERVICE

Head Office
Cliff Hill House, 3 Sandy Walk, Wakefield WF1 2DJ. Telephone 01924 364141.

Local Offices
57 Ferrybridge Road, Castleford WF10 4JW. Telephone 01977 558358.
Harropwell Lane, Pontefract WF8 1QY. Telephone 01977 791357.
20-30 Lawefield Lane, Wakefield WF2 8SP. Telephone 01924 361156.

YORKSHIRE WATER

Bill Enquiries: Telephone 0345 828889.
Sewerage Enquiries: Telephone 0345 828886.
Water Supply: Telephone 0345 828888.

YOUTH SERVICE

Computer Block
Room 433, County Hall, Wakefield WF1 2QW. Telephone 01924 305544.

STATISTICAL INFORMATION

Population	
	317,100
Area	83,670 acres
	33,860 hectares
	130.7 sq miles
Number of domestic premises (February 1997)	132,548
Number of Council Houses (February 1997)	38,908

Wakefield
CITY CENTRE PARTNERSHIP

A dynamic new partnership between the private, public and voluntary sectors of Wakefield

Achievements - the Partnership promotes

- New city centre events and street entertainment
- City centre CCTV
- European funding for redevelopment projects
- City Centre clean-ups - graffiti, flyposting and litter
- The Wakefield in Bloom Floral Campaign
- Marketing and promotions for city centre shopping and leisure
- City centre security initiatives
- Increased business participation and new partnerships...*and lots more!*

Find out more about the Partnership's exciting new plans and project opportunities by contacting

The City Centre Manager
Wakefield City Centre Partnership
1 Marygate, Wakefield,
West Yorkshire WF1 1PA

Telephone 01924 215181
Facsimile 01924 215182

Making the most of your city

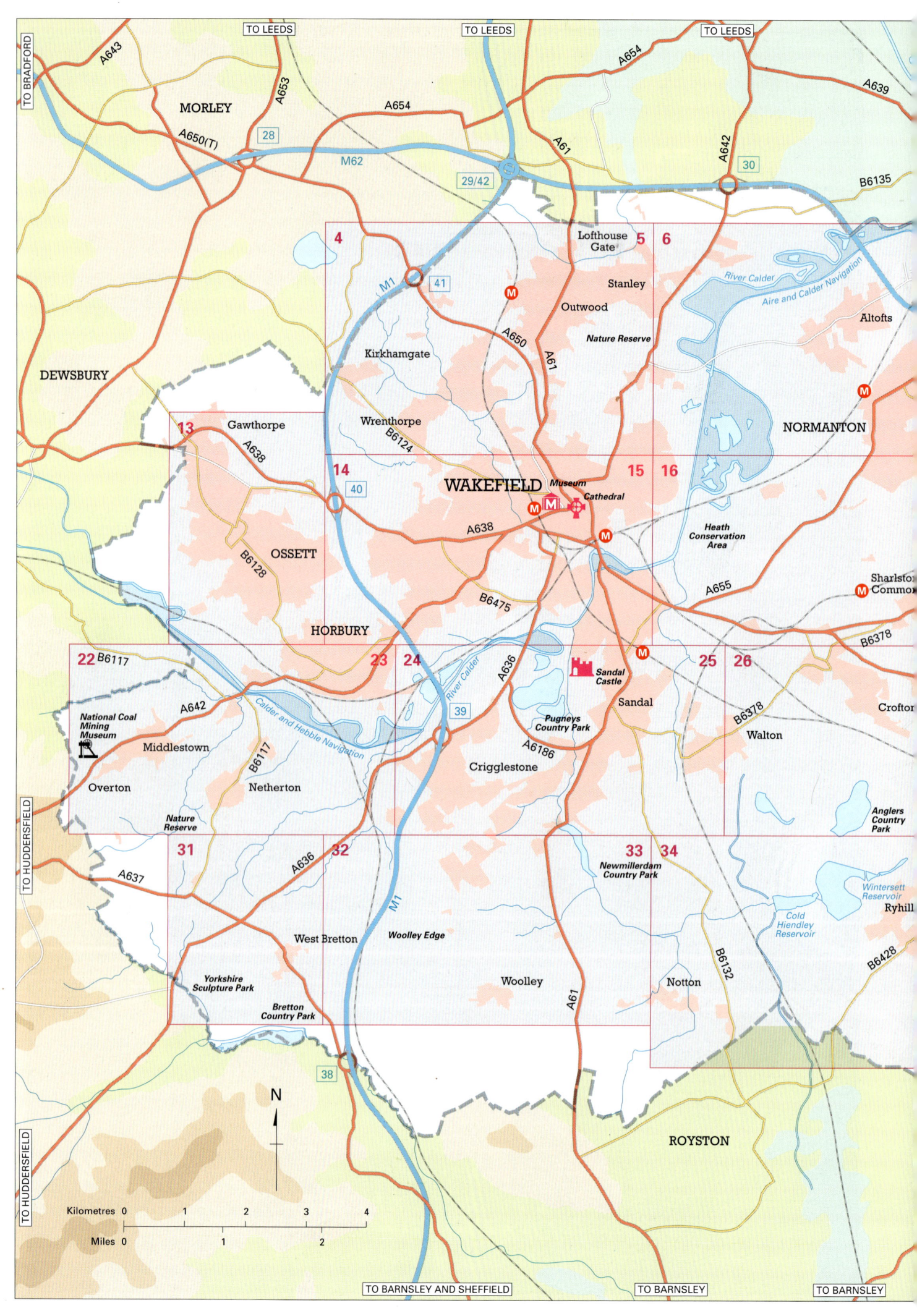

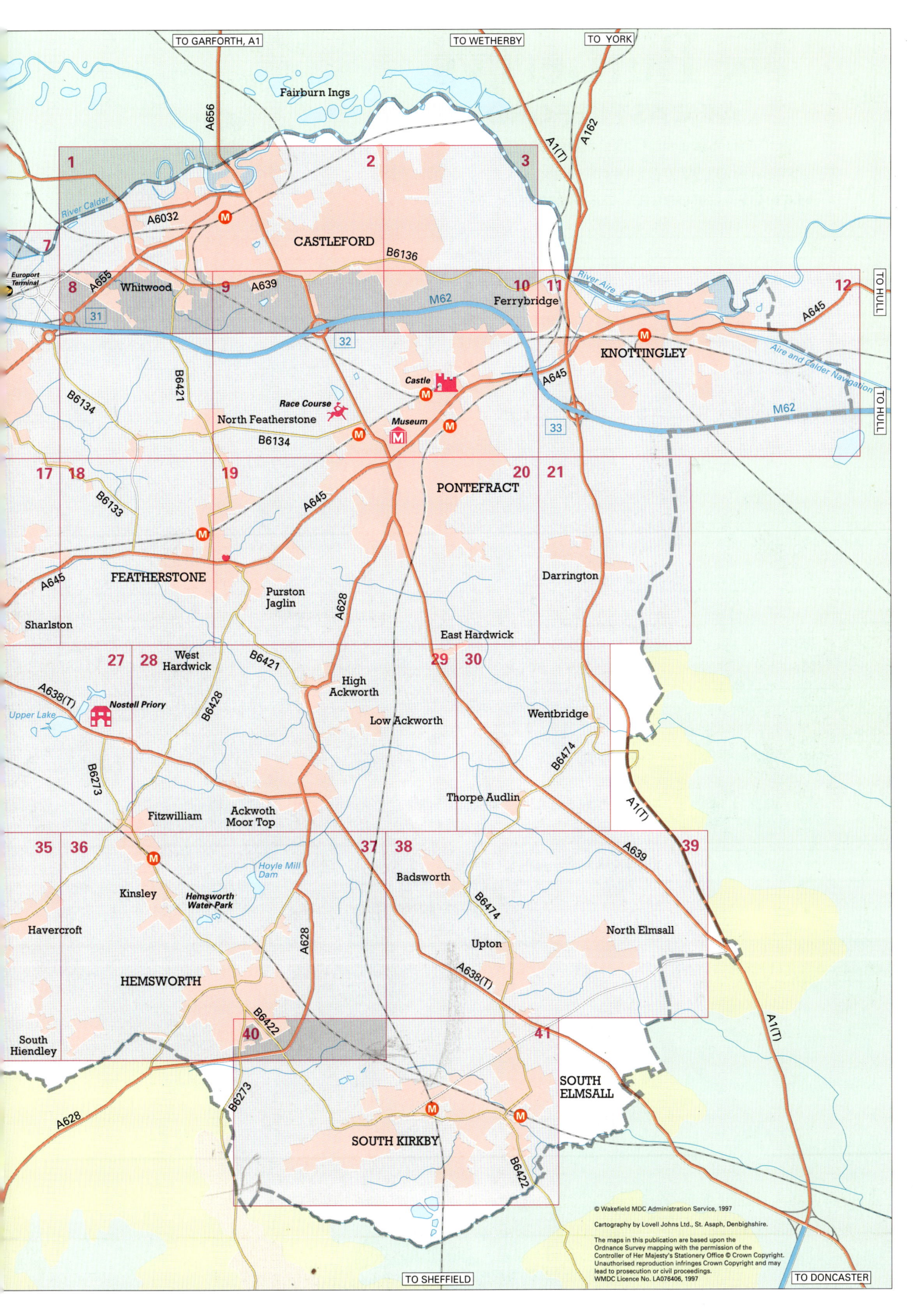

Burberrys
AT CASTLEFORD

Albion Street, Castleford, WF10 1QX
Telephone: 01977 554411 Fax: 01977 551472

MANUFACTURERS OF FINE CLOTHING

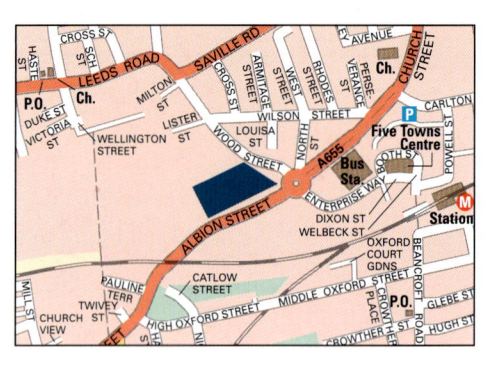

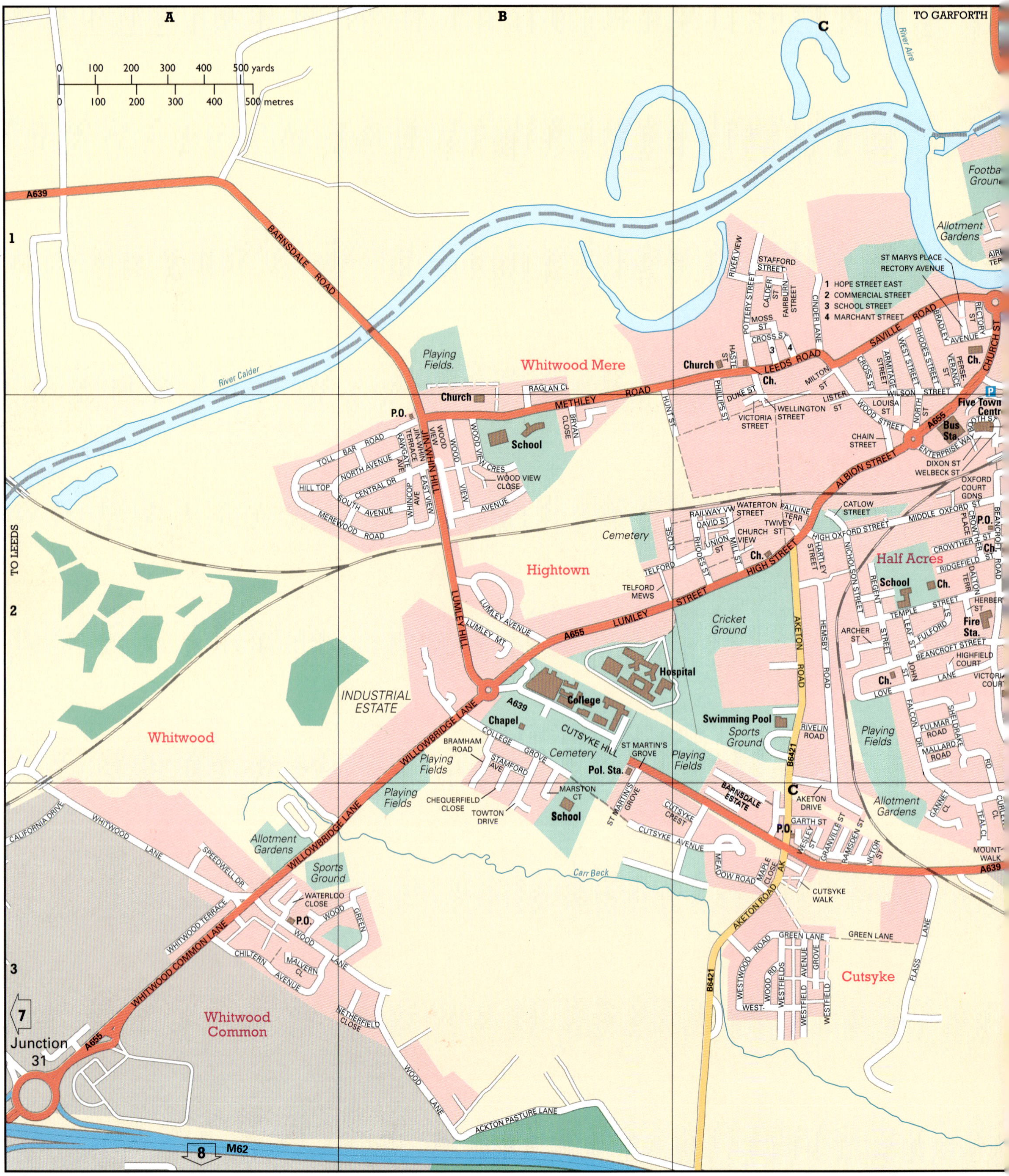

HICKSON
Hickson & Welch Ltd.
Organic Chemical Manufacturers

Wheldon Road
Castleford
West Yorkshire
WF10 2JT
Tel: (01977) 556565
Fax (01977) 518058

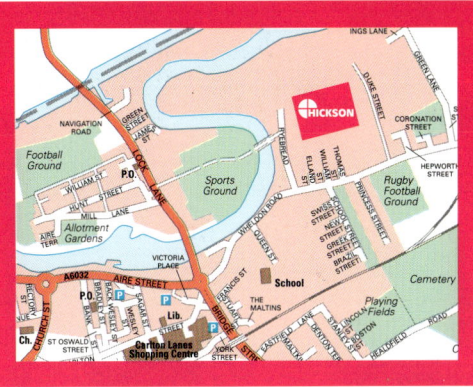

Carlton Lanes Shopping Centre Castleford

We've got your shopping covered!

Customer Care Line **01977 603338**

CARLTON LANES

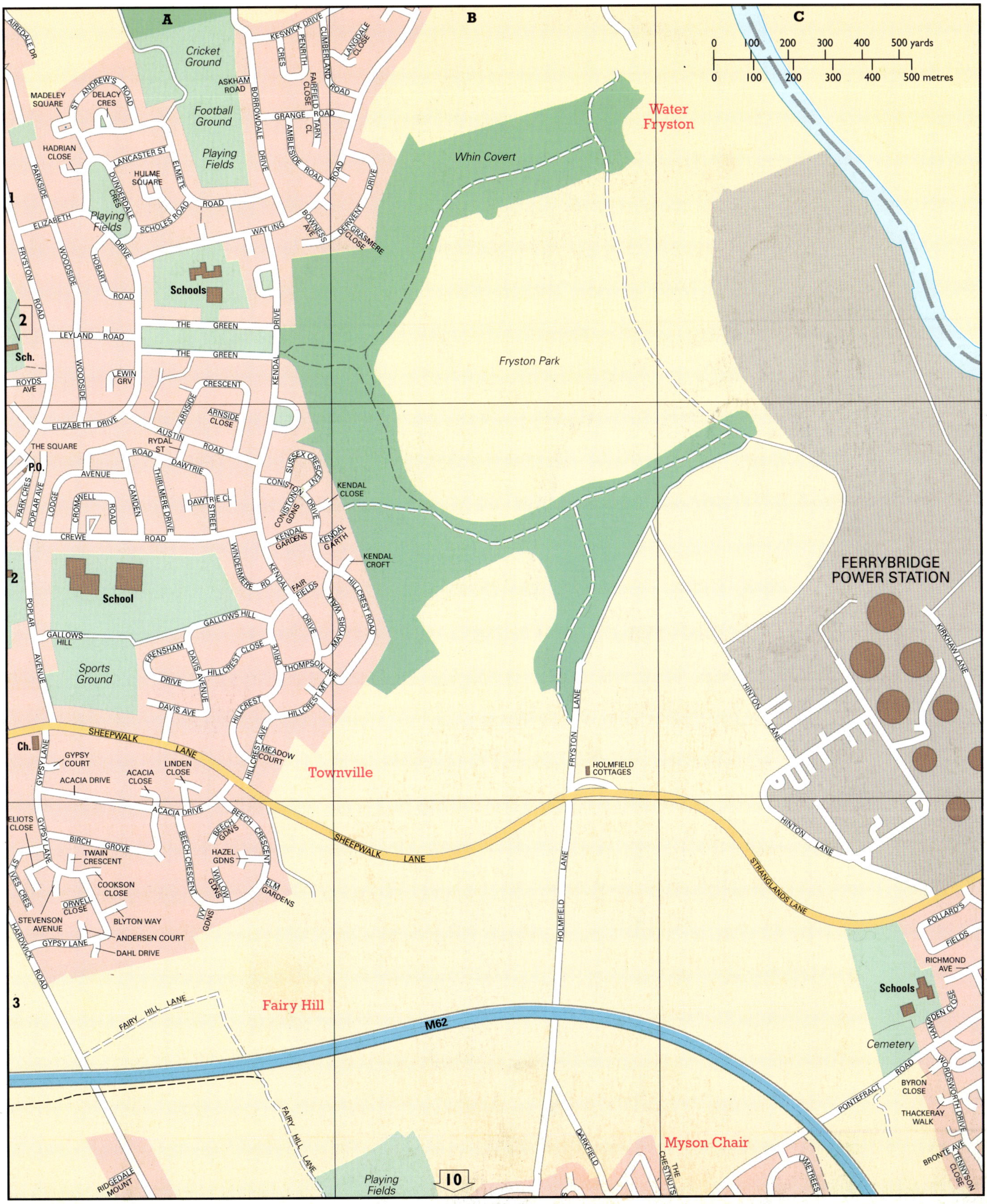

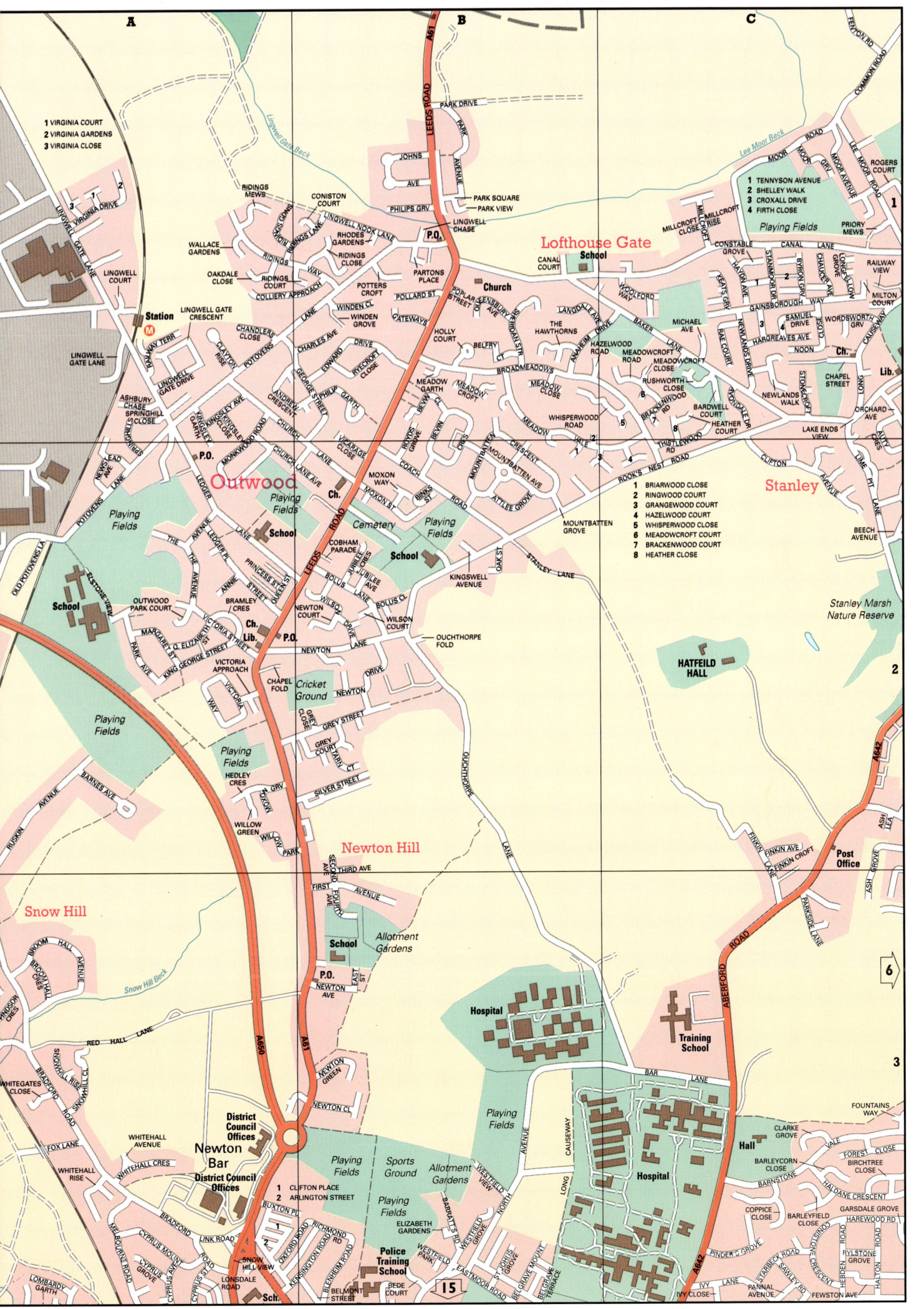

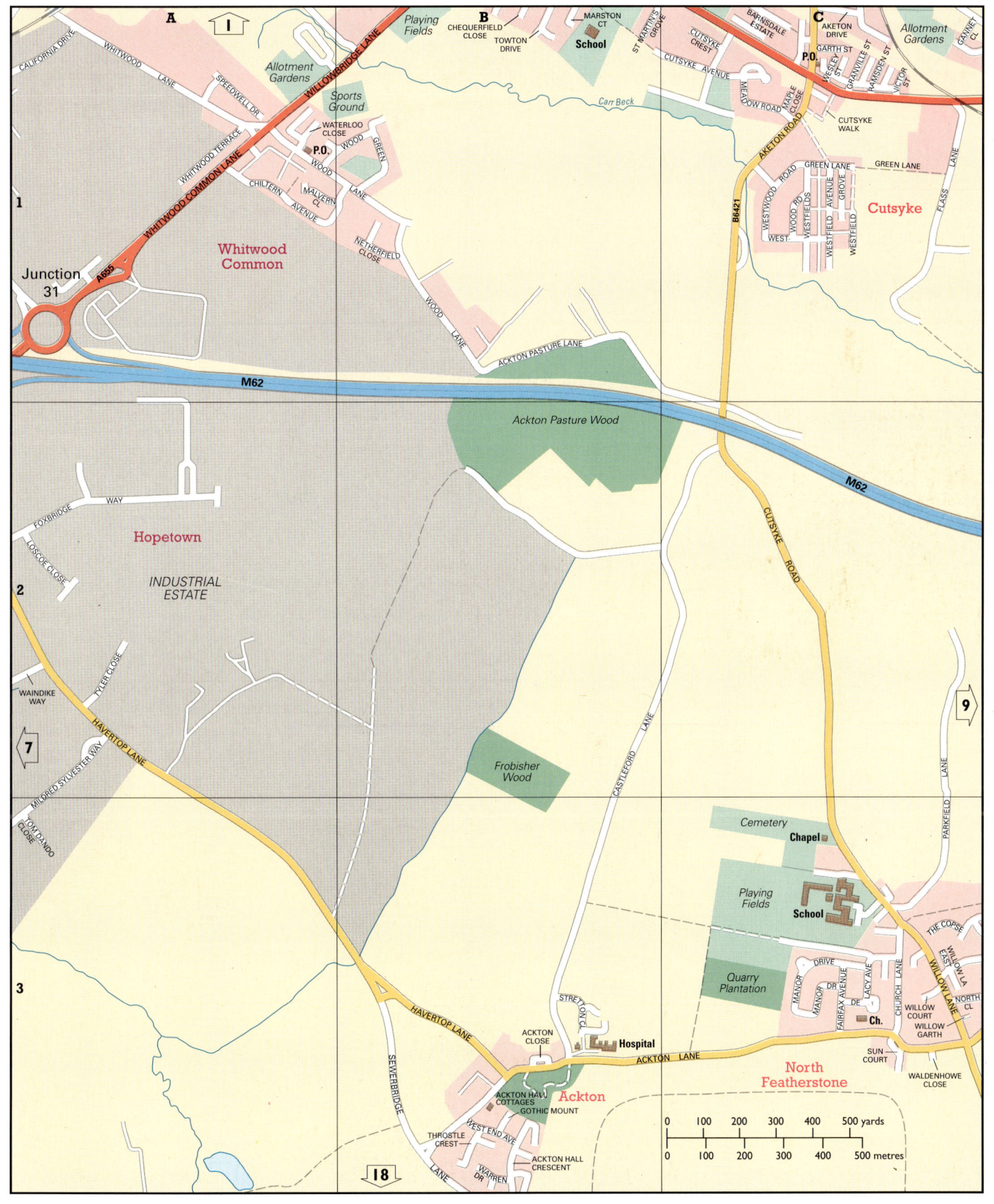

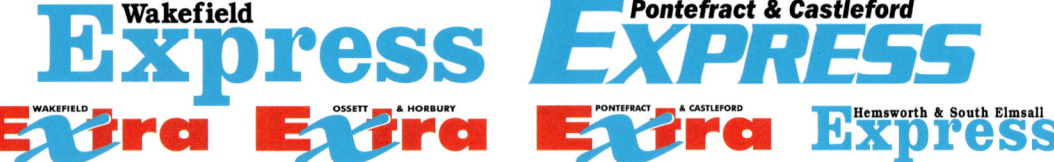

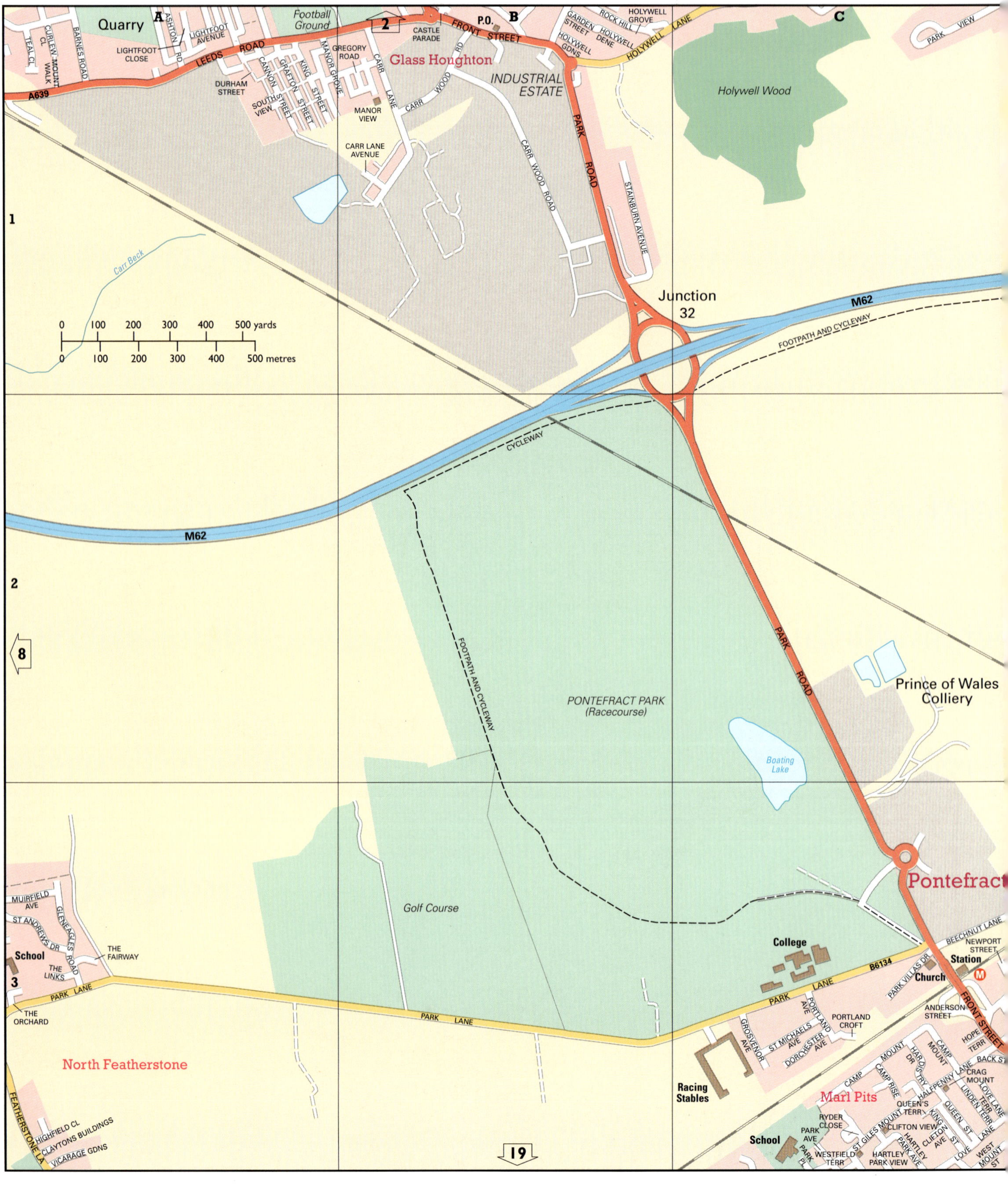

A
B
C
1
2
3
2
8
19
Quarry
Football Ground
Glass Houghton
INDUSTRIAL ESTATE
P.O.
CASTLE PARADE
FRONT STREET
LEEDS ROAD
A639
LIGHTFOOT CLOSE
LIGHTFOOT AVENUE
ASHTON RD
BARNES ROAD
CURLEW MOUNT
CURLEW CL
TEAL CL
WALK
DURHAM STREET
CANNON STREET
SOUTH VIEW
GRAFTON STREET
KING STREET
MANOR GROVE
GREGORY ROAD
MANOR VIEW
CARR LANE
CARR WOOD RD
CARR LANE AVENUE
CARR WOOD ROAD
PARK ROAD
STAINBURN AVENUE
GARDEN STREET
ROCK HILL
HOLYWELL GROVE
HOLYWELL DENE
HOLYWELL GDNS
HOLYWELL LANE
PARK VIEW
Holywell Wood
Carr Beck
0 100 200 300 400 500 yards
0 100 200 300 400 500 metres
Junction 32
M62
FOOTPATH AND CYCLEWAY
CYCLEWAY
PONTEFRACT PARK
(Racecourse)
Prince of Wales Colliery
Boating Lake
Golf Course
Pontefract
College
Station
Church
B6134
PARK LANE
PARK VILLAS DR
BEECHNUT LANE
NEWPORT STREET
FRONT STREET
ANDERSON STREET
PORTLAND AVE
PORTLAND CROFT
GROSVENOR AVE
ST MICHAELS AVE
DORCHESTER AVE
Racing Stables
Marl Pits
CAMP MOUNT
CAMP RISE
HARDY DR
HALFPENNY LANE
HOPE TERR
BACK ST
CRAG MOUNT
LINDEN TERR
LOVE LANE TERR
QUEEN'S TERR
CLIFTON VIEW
KING ST
QUEEN ST
CLIFTON AVE
HARTLEY PARK AVE
HARTLEY PARK VIEW
WESTFIELD TERR
ST GILES MOUNT
RYDER CLOSE
PARK AVE
PARK PL
LOVE LANE
WEST MOUNT ST
School
MUIRFIELD AVE
ST ANDREWS DR
GLENEAGLES ROAD
THE FAIRWAY
THE LINKS
THE ORCHARD
North Featherstone
FEATHERSTONE LA
HIGHFIELD CL
CLAYTONS BUILDINGS
VICARAGE GDNS

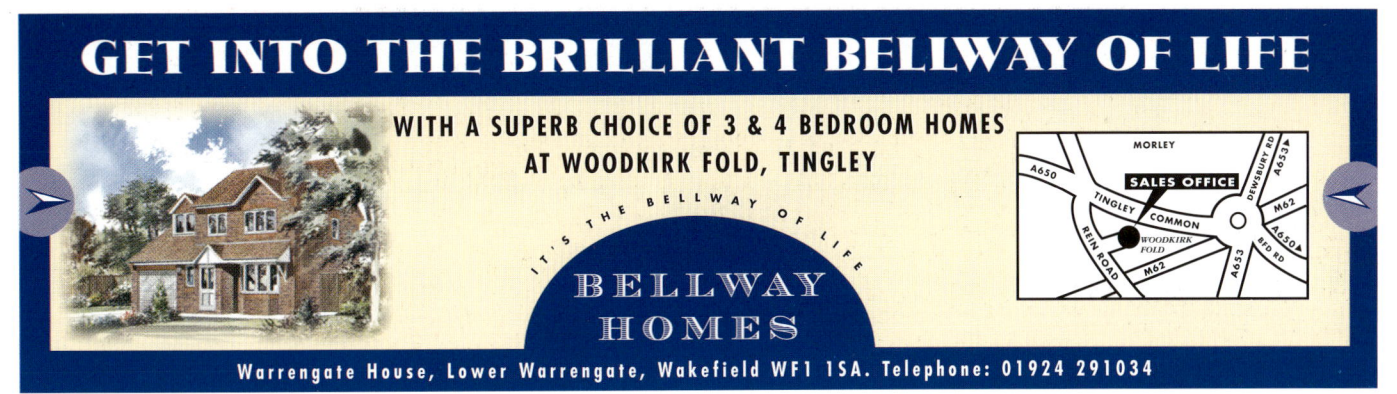

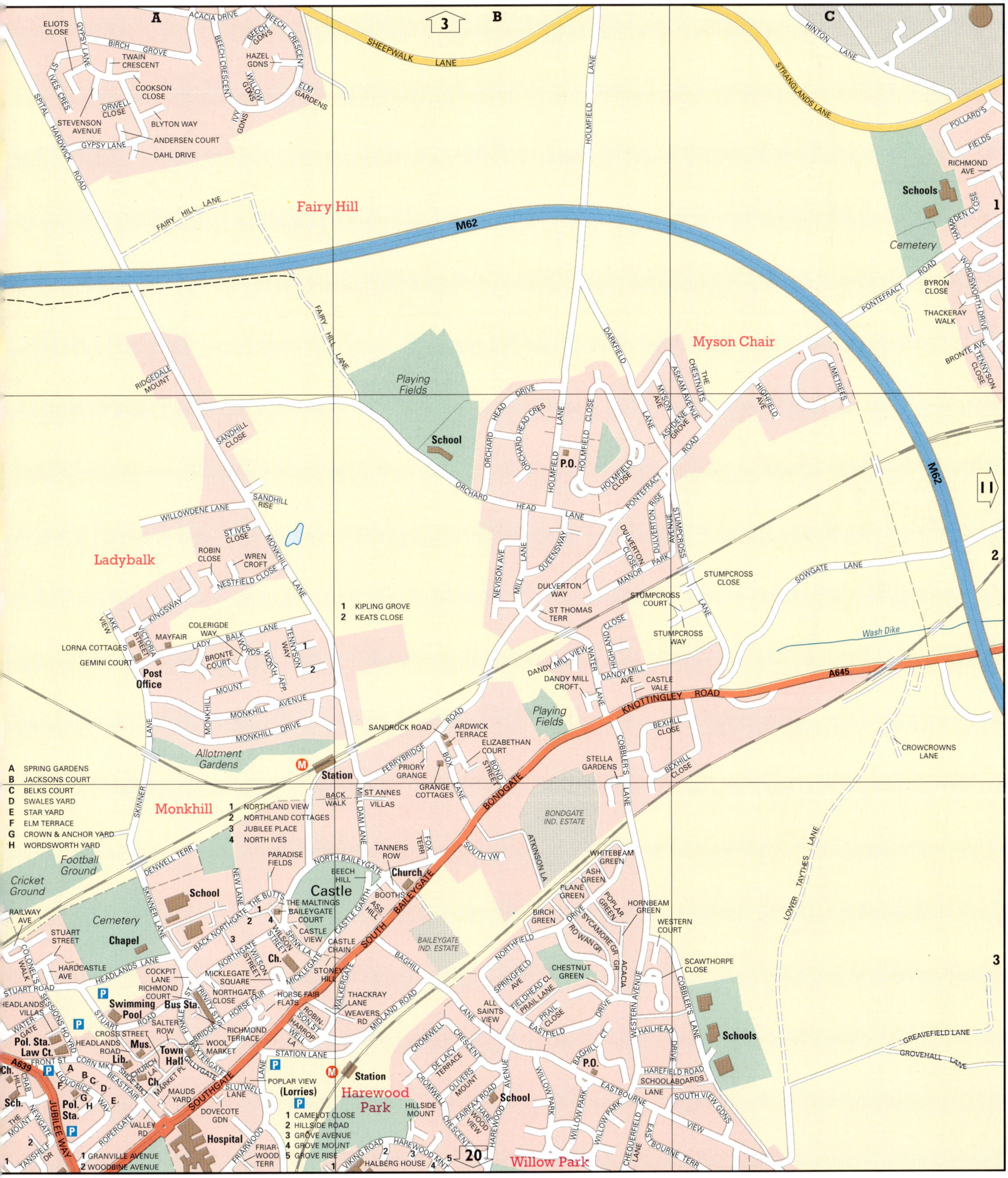

A
B
C
3
11
20
1
2
3
Fairy Hill
Myson Chair
Ladybalk
Monkhill
Harewood Park
Willow Park
M62
A645
A639
SHEEPWALK LANE
STRANGLANDS LANE
HINTON LANE
HOLMFIELD LANE
FAIRY HILL LANE
SPITAL HARDWICK ROAD
ACACIA DRIVE
BEECH CRESCENT
ELIOTS CLOSE
GYPSY LANE
BIRCH GROVE
TWAIN CRESCENT
COOKSON CLOSE
ORWELL CLOSE
STEVENSON AVENUE
BLYTON WAY
ANDERSEN COURT
DAHL DRIVE
POLLARD'S FIELDS
RICHMOND AVE
Schools
Cemetery
BYRON CLOSE
THACKERAY WALK
WORDSWORTH DRIVE
BRONTE AVE
TENNYSON CLOSE
PONTEFRACT ROAD
Playing Fields
School
P.O.
ORCHARD HEAD DRIVE
ORCHARD HEAD CRES
ORCHARD HEAD LANE
HOLMFIELD CLOSE
DARKFIELD
ASKHAM AVENUE
THE CHESTNUTS
HIGHFIELD AVE
LIMETREES
RIDGEDALE MOUNT
SANDHILL CLOSE
SANDHILL RISE
WILLOWDENE LANE
ST IVES CLOSE
ROBIN CLOSE
WREN CROFT
NESTFIELD CLOSE
MONKHILL LANE
KINGSWAY
QUEENSWAY
NEVISON AVE
MILL LANE
DULVERTON WAY
DULVERTON CLOSE
DULVERTON RISE
STUMPCROSS LANE
STUMPCROSS CLOSE
STUMPCROSS COURT
STUMPCROSS WAY
SOWGATE LANE
Wash Dike
ST THOMAS TERR
1 KIPLING GROVE
2 KEATS CLOSE
COLERIDGE WAY
LORNA COTTAGES
GEMINI COURT
Post Office
MAYFAIR
BRONTE COURT
TENNYSON WAY
MONKHILL AVENUE
MONKHILL DRIVE
MONKHILL MOUNT
DANDY MILL VIEW
DANDY MILL CROFT
DANDY MILL AVE
CASTLE VALE
KNOTTINGLEY ROAD
BEXHILL CLOSE
CROWCROWNS LANE
SANDROCK ROAD
ARDWICK TERRACE
ELIZABETHAN COURT
Allotment Gardens
Station
PRIORY GRANGE
GRANGE COTTAGES
STELLA GARDENS
COBBLERS LANE
A SPRING GARDENS
B JACKSONS COURT
C BELKS COURT
D SWALES YARD
E STAR YARD
F ELM TERRACE
G CROWN & ANCHOR YARD
H WORDSWORTH YARD
1 NORTHLAND VIEW
2 NORTHLAND COTTAGES
3 JUBILEE PLACE
4 NORTH IVES
BACK WALK
ST ANNES VILLAS
BONDGATE
BONDGATE IND. ESTATE
LOWER TAYTHES LANE
Football Ground
Cricket Ground
SKINNER LANE
DENWELL TERR
PARADISE FIELDS
TANNERS ROW
Church
SOUTH VW
ATKINSON LA
WHITEBEAM GREEN
ASH GREEN
PLANE GREEN
HORNBEAM GREEN
WESTERN COURT
School
Castle
NORTH BAILEYGATE
THE MALTINGS
BAILEYGATE COURT
CASTLE VIEW
CASTLE CHAIN
BAILEYGATE IND. ESTATE
SOUTH BAILEYGATE
Cemetery
Chapel
RAILWAY AVE
STUART STREET
HARDCASTLE AVE
HEADLANDS LANE
COCKPIT LANE
RICHMOND COURT
MICKLEGATE SQUARE
NORTHGATE CLOSE
STUART ROAD
HEADLANDS VILLAS
Swimming Pool
Bus Sta.
HORSE FAIR FLATS
THACKRAY LANE
WEAVERS RD
MIDLAND ROAD
SCAWTHORPE CLOSE
CHESTNUT GREEN
Schools
GREAVEFIELD LANE
GROVEHALL LANE
Pol. Sta.
Law Ct.
Mus.
Town Hall
Lib.
Ch.
RICHMOND TERRACE
WOOL MARKET
SALTER ROW
CROSS STREET
STATION LANE
Station
POPLAR VIEW (Lorries)
DOVECOTE GDN
Hospital
1 CAMELOT CLOSE
2 HILLSIDE ROAD
3 GROVE AVENUE
4 GROVE MOUNT
5 GROVE RISE
HILLSIDE MOUNT
School
HAREFIELD ROAD
SCHOOLBOARDS LANE
SOUTH VIEW GDNS
EASTBOURNE VIEW
EASTBOURNE TERR
CHEQUERFIELD LANE
WILLOW PARK
1 GRANVILLE AVENUE
2 WOODBINE AVENUE
HALBERG HOUSE
VIKING ROAD
JUBILEE WAY

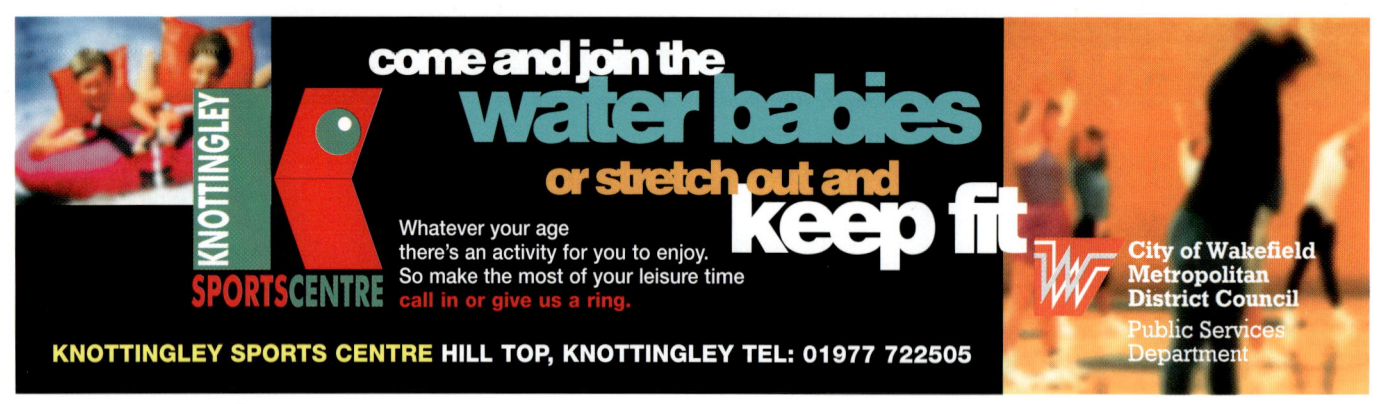

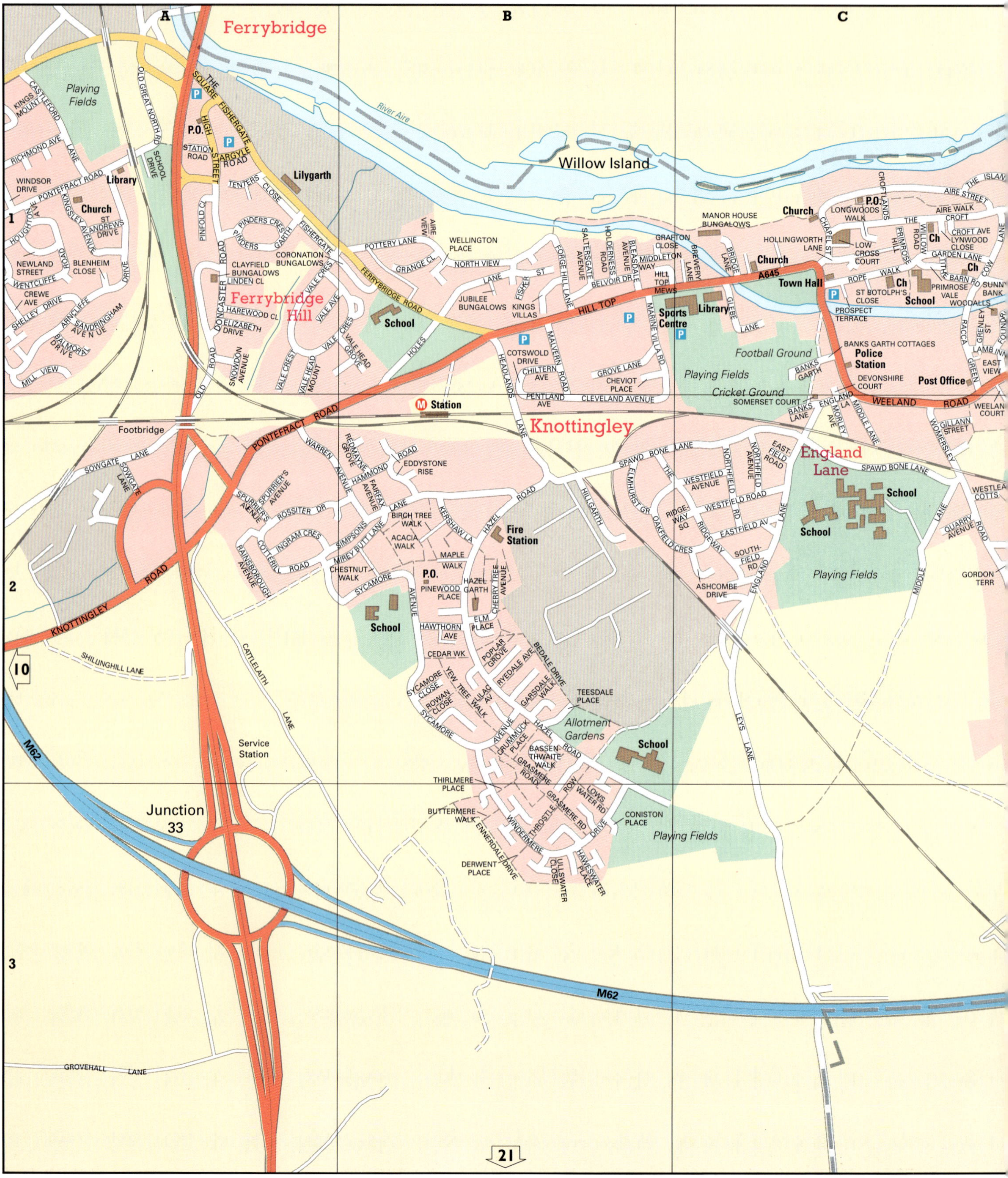

A
B
C
1
2
3
Ferrybridge
River Aire
Willow Island
Lilygarth
Playing Fields
Library
Church
Ferrybridge Hill
School
Station
Footbridge
Knottingley
Sports Centre
Town Hall
Football Ground
Playing Fields
Cricket Ground
Police Station
Post Office
England Lane
School
Fire Station
P.O.
Allotment Gardens
Playing Fields
Service Station
Junction 33
M62
10
21
PONTEFRACT ROAD
HILL TOP
A645
WEELAND ROAD
KNOTTINGLEY ROAD
FERRYBRIDGE ROAD
SPAWD BONE LANE
SHILLINGHILL LANE
CATTLELAITH LANE
LEYS LANE
GROVEHALL LANE
SOWGATE LANE
HEADLANDS LANE
HILLGARTH

PRESTON SECURITY SERVICES

- Static & Mobile patrols
- Emergency cover provided
- 24 hour service - 365 days a year
- Fully insured
- Smart uniformed staff
- Key handling / Alarm response
- All types of premises covered

Clients include: Wakefield District Council, Norweb, YTV, Powergen, Yorkshire Water

Telephone 01924 826035/01924 828943. Fax 01924 828747.

SECURITY TO SUIT YOUR BUDGET
18 GREY STREET, OUTWOOD, WAKEFIELD WF1 3HQ

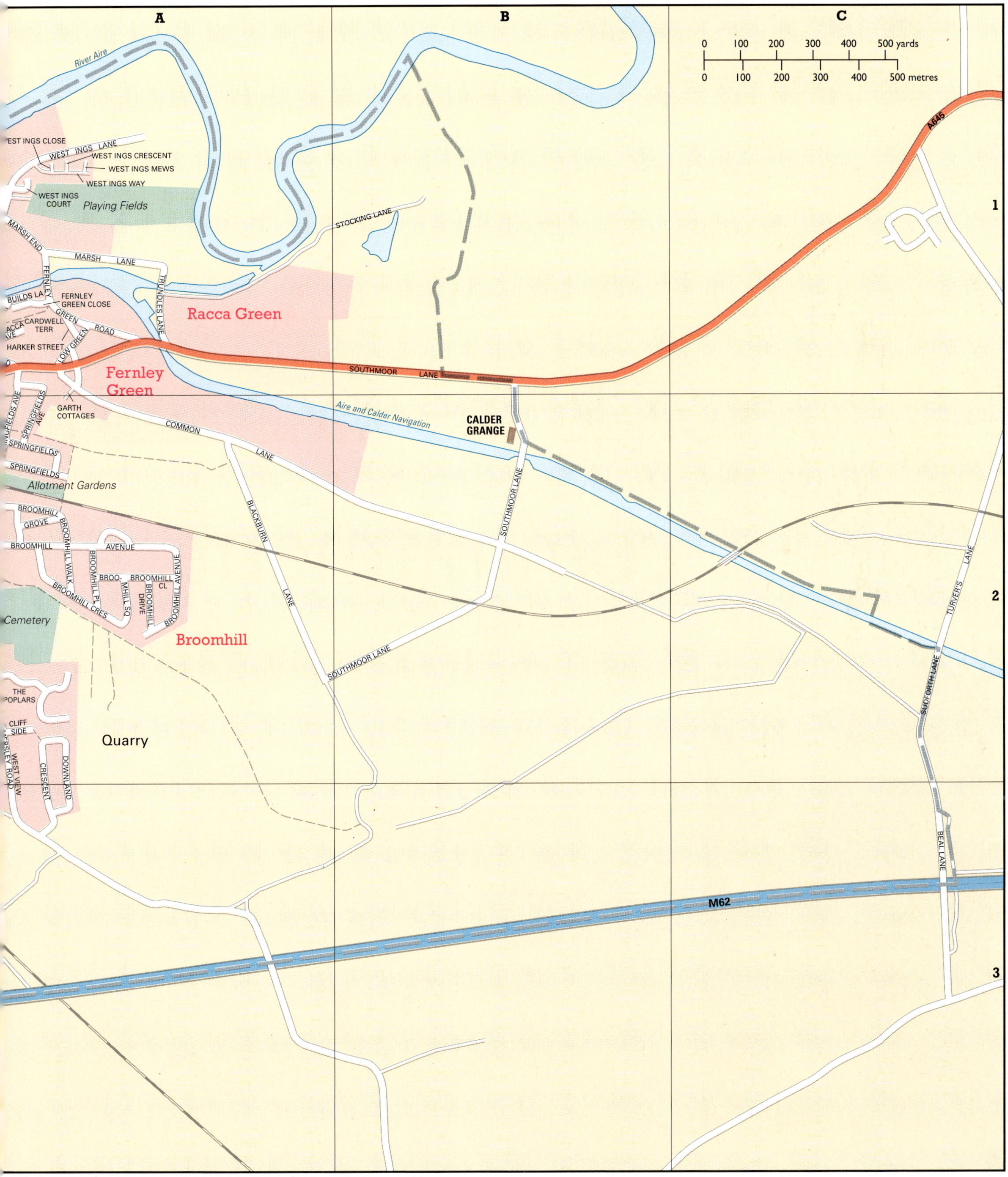

We can help with

- Business Advice
- European Services
- Community Employment Projects
- Conference Venues and Tourism
- Planning Advice
- Building Control Advice
- Town Centre Management
- Managed Workspace and Training
- Business Premises and Sites
- Engineering Division
- Highway Maintenance and Design
- Traffic Management
- District Maps
- Car Parks

Working together
to provide you
with the best service is part of our
commitment
to the development
of our community

For a free service please contact

The Regeneration Department
Newton Bar
Leeds Road
Wakefield
West Yorkshire
WF1 2TX

Tel: 01924 306636
Fax 01924 306690

**City of Wakefield
Metropolitan District Council**
Regeneration Department

Come and dine in style
at the Clock Tower Restaurant

We offer a different evening menu each weekend with a choice of traditional and international dishes

Enjoy seriously good food in comfortable and elegant surroundings

Monday - Friday
LUNCHTIME MENU
MORNING COFFEE
AFTERNOON TEA

Friday and Saturday
WEEKEND DINING
SUNDAY LUNCH

UNDER THE
CLOCK TOWER
TOWN HALL
WOOD STREET
WAKEFIELD
WF1 2HQ

UNDER THE CLOCK TOWER

Restaurant 01924 305130   **Weddings & Conferences** 01924 305121

cobra RAILFREIGHT LTD

PRIVATE RAIL TERMINAL FOR THE WAKEFIELD AREA
HANDLING, WAREHOUSING & ROAD LINK FACILITIES

Calder Vale Road, Wakefield WF1 5PE Telephone (01924) 375838 Facsimile (01924) 371923

track down some action

TRAINING ATHLETICS
AEROBICS CRECHE
AND LOTS MORE!!

THORNES PARK ATHLETICS STADIUM, Horbury Road, Wakefield. Tel: 01924 302385

City of Wakefield Metropolitan District Council
Public Services Department

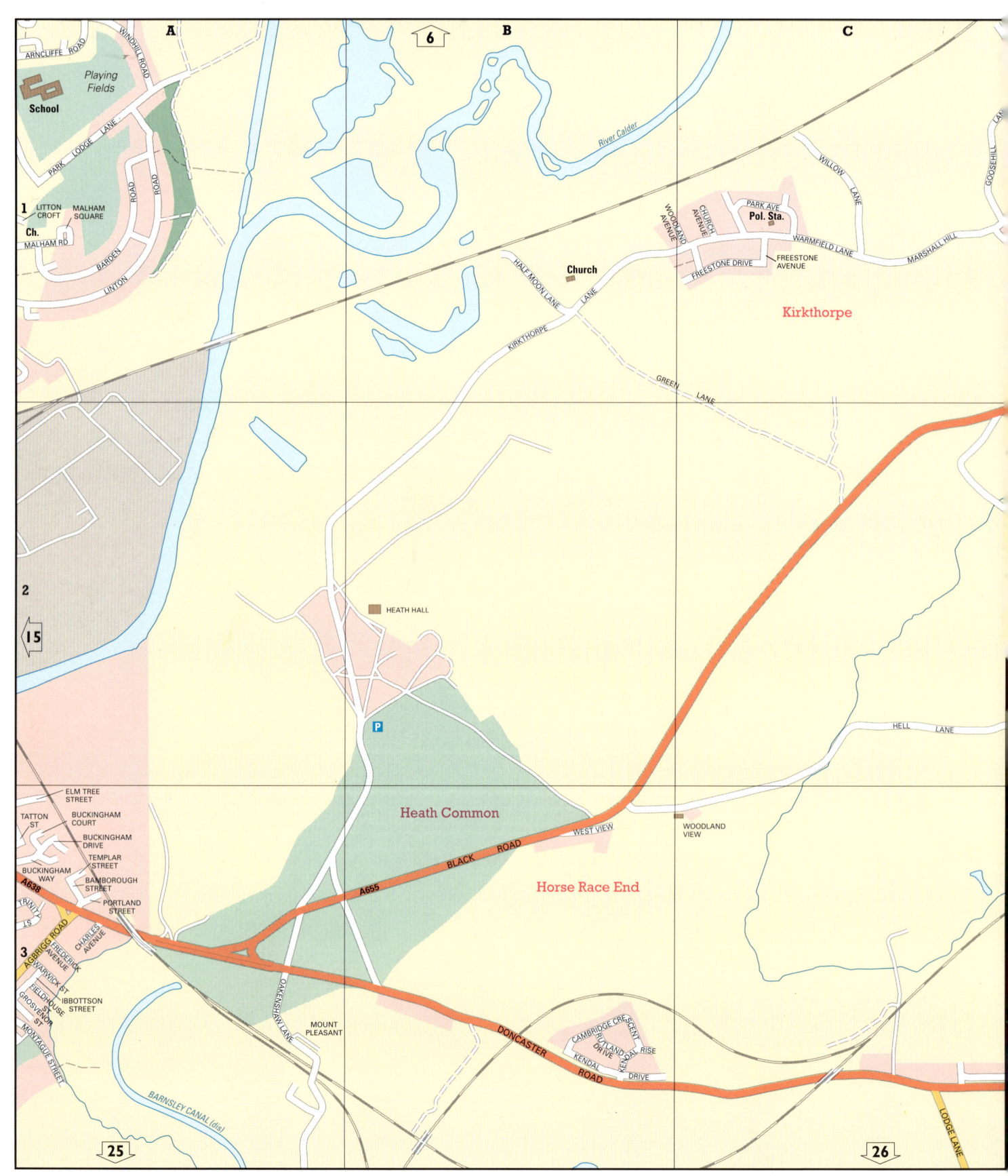

Come along to Wakefield's first Cyber Access Point

WINDOWS 95
MICROSOFT OFFICE 95

SURF THE NET
ELECTRONIC MAIL

CYBER CAFÉ — WAKEFIELD PONTEFRACT

Prospect Corner
25 Northgate Wakefield Tel: 01924 201818
Email: @wakefield.prospectcorner.co.uk

Prospect Corner
9 Market Place Pontefract Tel: 01977 602292
Email: @pontefract.prospectcorner.co.uk

17

CASTLEFORD SWIMMING POOL
AKETON ROAD
CASTLEFORD
TEL 01977 722055

FEATHERSTONE SWIMMING POOL
LISTER ROAD
FEATHERSTONE
TEL 01977 722710

MINSTHORPE SWIMMING POOL
ASH GROVE
SOUTH ELMSALL
TEL 01977 642018

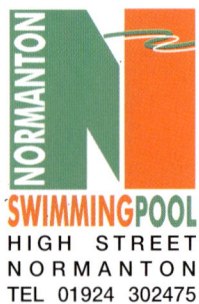

NORMANTON SWIMMING POOL
HIGH STREET
NORMANTON
TEL 01924 302475

PONTEFRACT SWIMMING POOL
STUART ROAD
PONTEFRACT
TEL 01977 722755

SUN LANE SWIMMING POOL
WAKEFIELD
TEL 01924 302370

go to any lengths for some action

For all round fitness and enjoyment, you can't beat a swim.

Family sessions, mums and toddlers, ante-natal classes, or learning the first strokes - we've got something for everyone to enjoy.

Find out what's on offer at your local pool now.

City of Wakefield Metropolitan District Council

Public Services Department

MARKETS
enjoy the experience

CASTLEFORD FEATHERSTONE HEMSWORTH NORMANTON OSSETT PONTEFRACT SOUTH ELMSALL WAKEFIELD

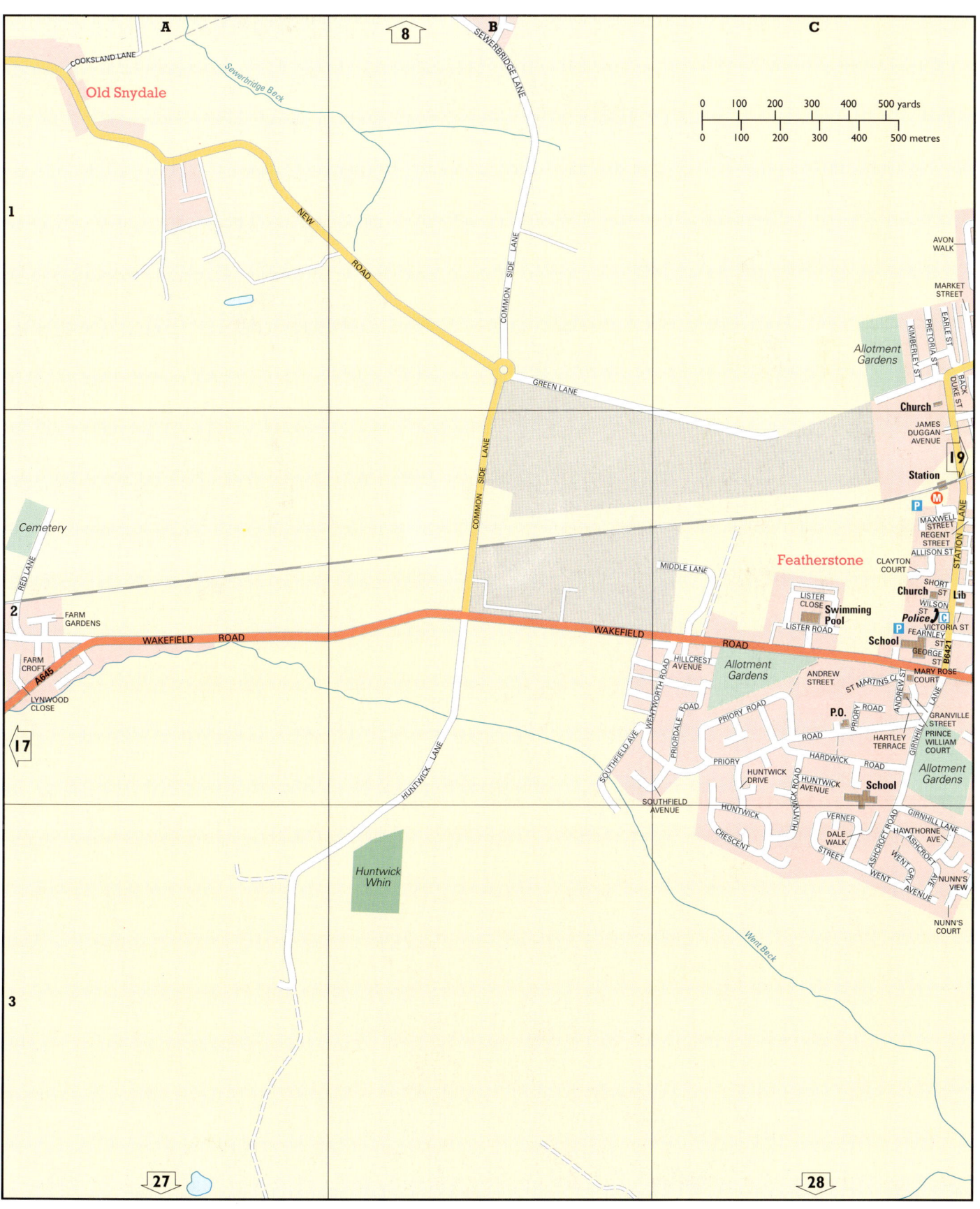

Conferences
at the Clock Tower

Our Conference and Seminar rooms, based in Wakefield's elegantly restored Victorian Town Hall, make the ideal venue whether you're planning the annual AGM, a prestigious product launch or a training seminar

We can offer state of the art audio visual equipment (including the latest videoconferencing and satellite facilities), specialist staff, the service of our superb Clock Tower Restaurant, all at an inclusive day delegate rate

For a FREE Conference Pack contact our conference co-ordinator
FREEPOST 458
TOWN HALL
WOOD STREET
WAKEFIELD
WF1 2HQ

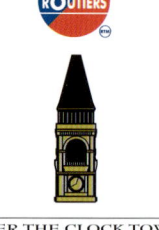

LES ROUTIERS

UNDER THE CLOCK TOWER

Under The Clock Tower 01924 305121

A
B
C
1
2
3
10
21
30
Eastbourne
Chequerfield
Carleton
East Hardwick
Infirmary
School
Church
P.O.
Ch.
Sch.
Allotment Gardens
Playing Fields
Rugby Ground
Fox Covert
Fletcher's Spring Covert
Little Went
MOOR BRIDGE
HUNDHILL HALL
NORWOOD
TUMBLING HILL
HALBERG HOUSE
TANSHELF DRIVE
A645
A639
MILL HILL ROAD
ACKWORTH ROAD
HARDWICK ROAD
CARLETON ROAD
MOOR LANE
GREEN LANE
FURLONG LANE
LONG LANE
BATES LANE
CHEQUERFIELD DRIVE
ROOKHILL ROAD
CHURCHBALK LANE
MONUMENT LANE
SCHOOL ROAD
EAST DRIVE
BROADWAY
EASTBOURNE VIEW
SPITALGAP LANE
STREET FURLONG LANE
DARRINGTON ROAD
WATER LANE
SANDY GATE LA
HUNDHILL LANE
WENSLEY DRIVE
THE WOODLANDS
BEECHLANDS
LILAC COTTAGES
THE ORCHARD
CARLETON GREEN STABLES
WESTFIELD COTTAGES
ROMAN RISE
WENT CROFT
SKELBROOKE DRIVE
BROOKE COURT
0 100 200 300 400 500 yards
0 100 200 300 400 500 metres

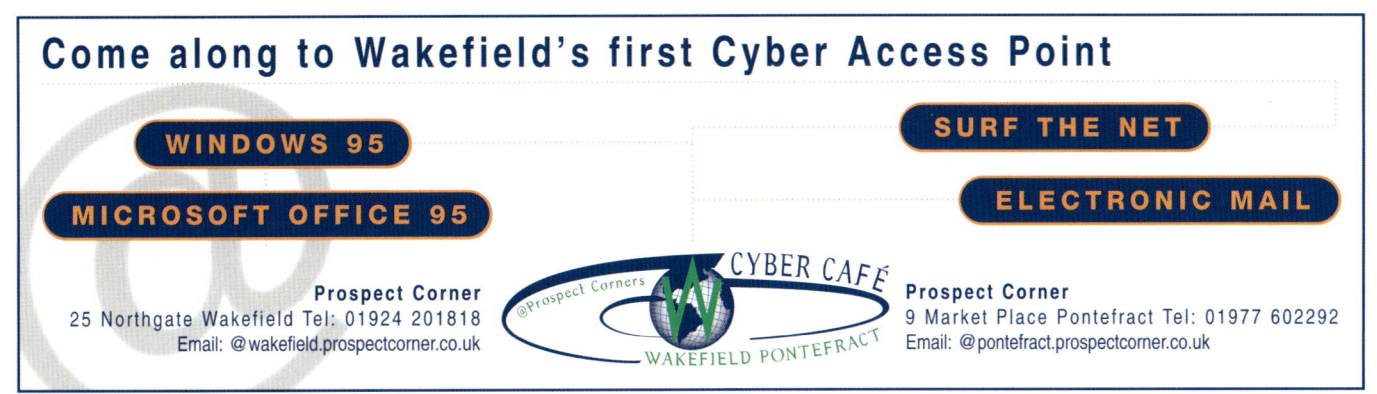

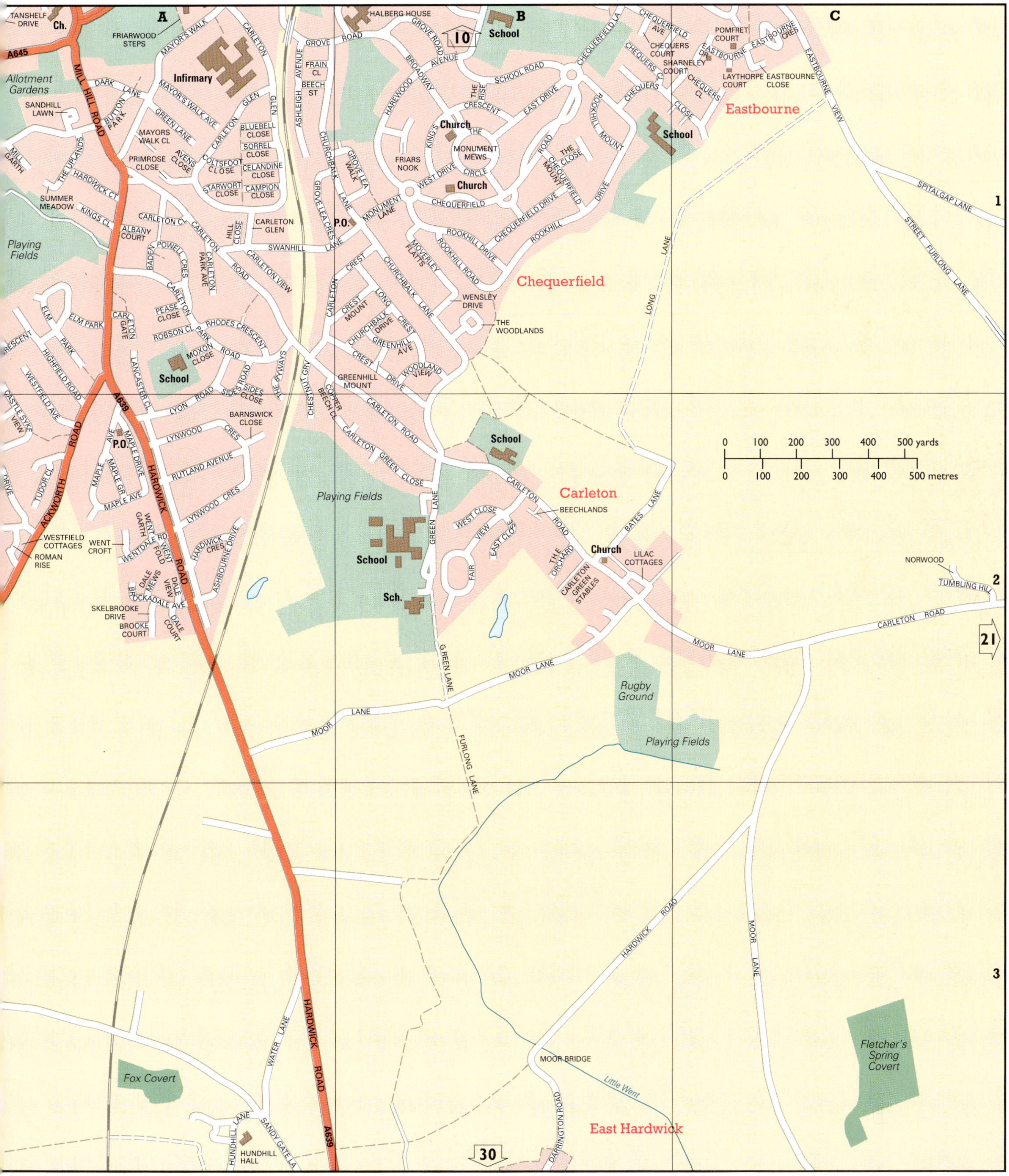

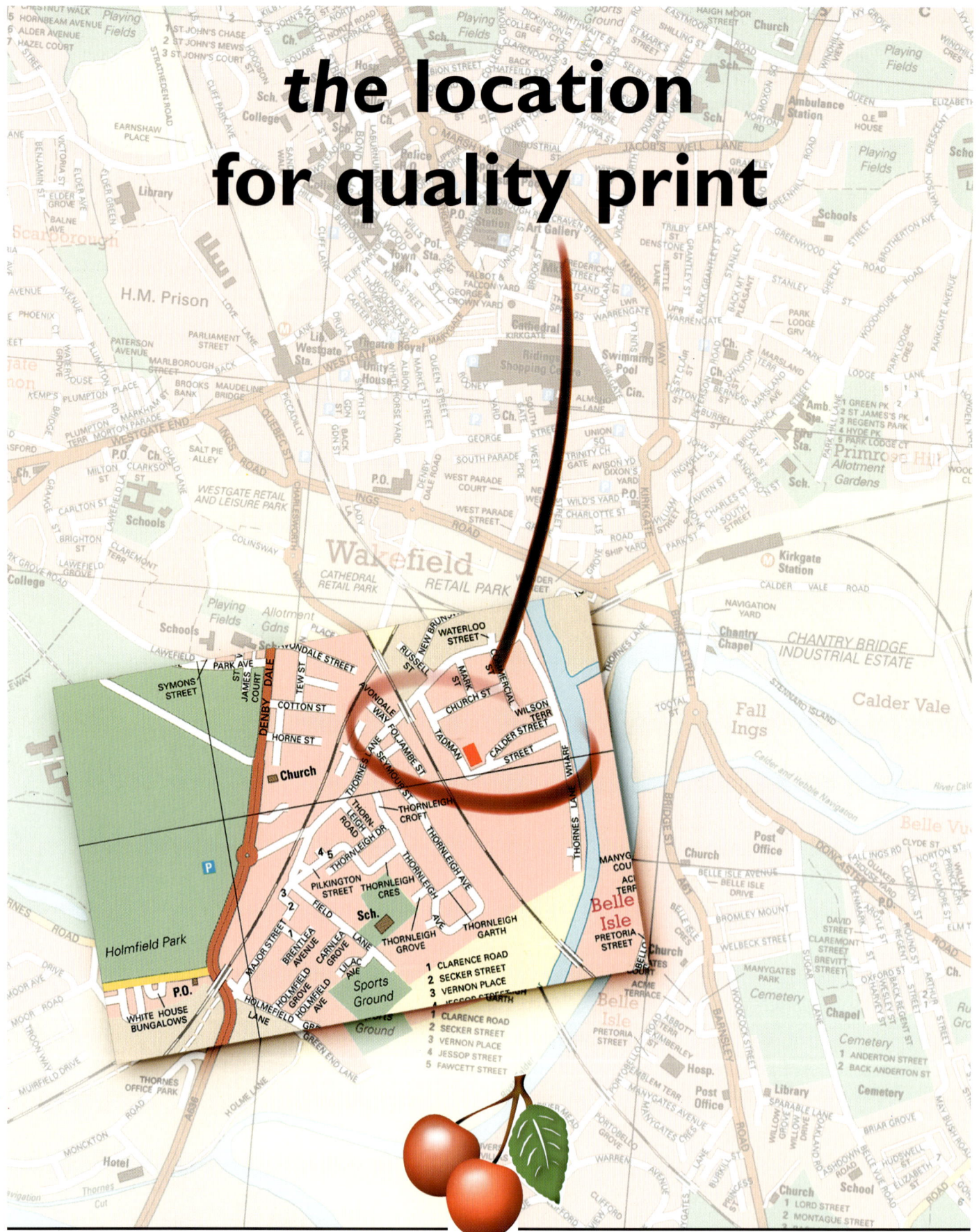

CHERRY PRINT LIMITED

3 Tadman Street, Wakefield, West Yorkshire WF1 5QU

Telephone: 01924 367805 • Fax: 01924 383146 • ISDN 01924 370432

e-mail cherryprint@ndirect.co.uk

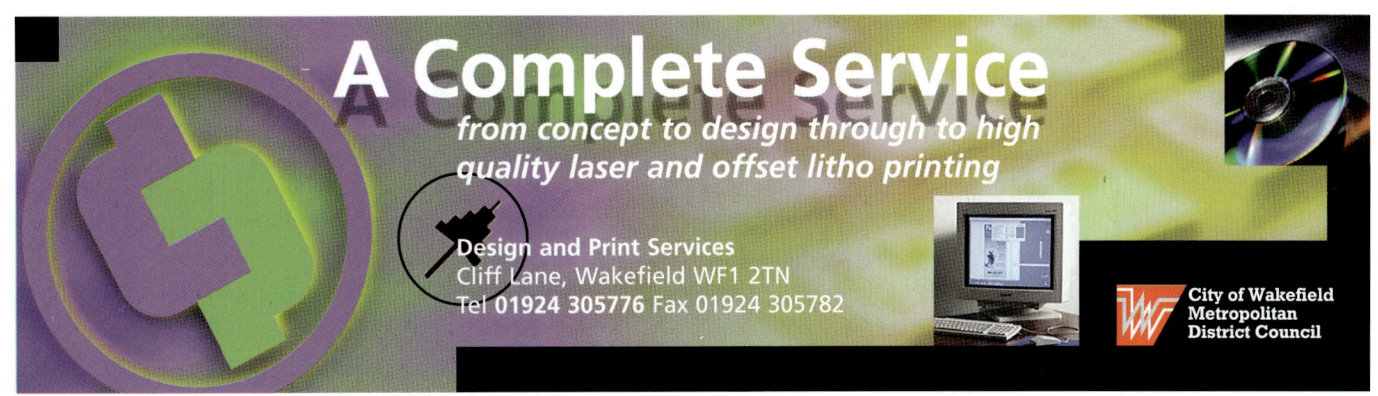

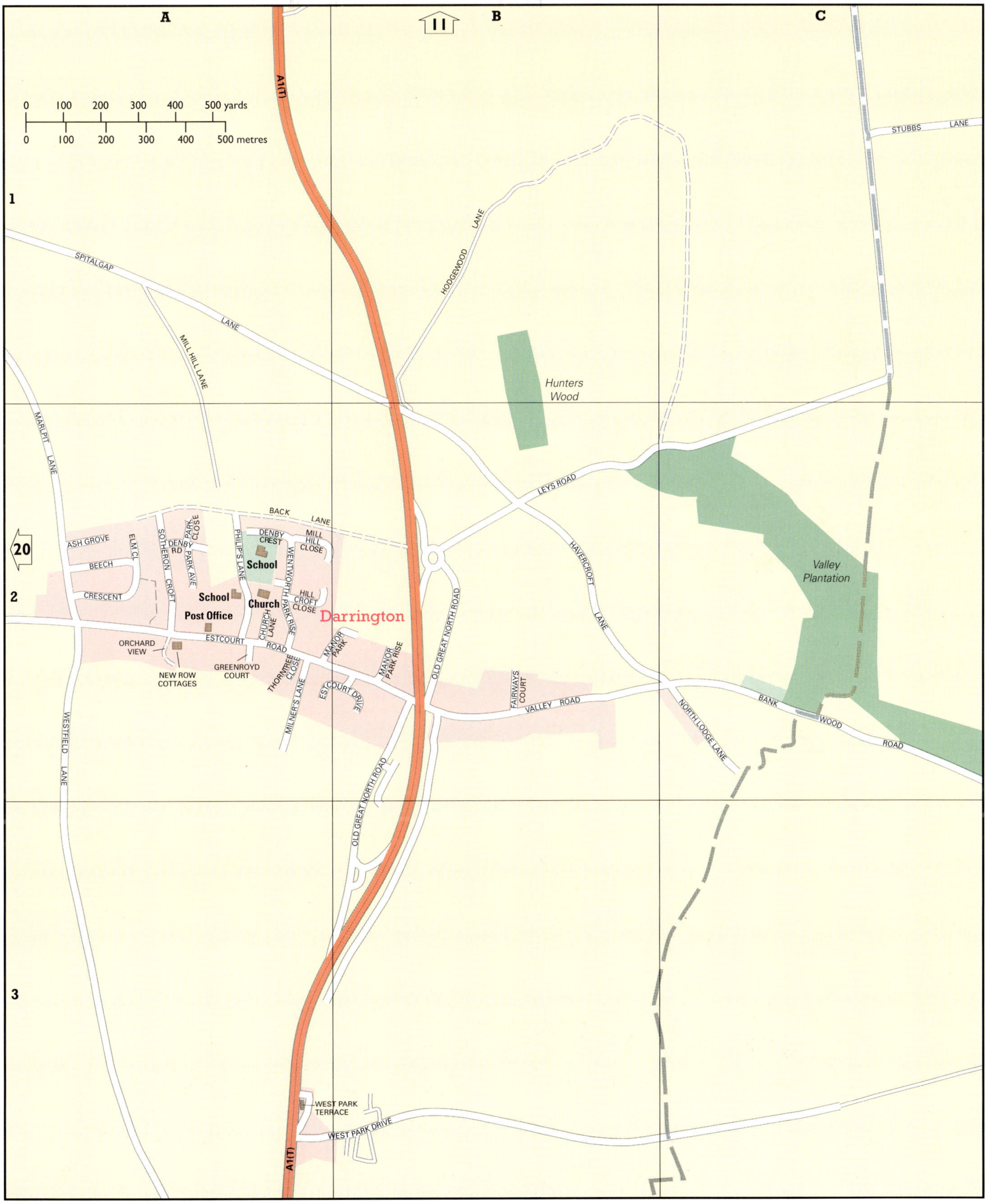
A
B
C
11
20
1
2
3
0 100 200 300 400 500 yards
0 100 200 300 400 500 metres
A1(T)
STUBBS LANE
HODGEWOOD LANE
SPITALGAP LANE
MILL HILL LANE
Hunters Wood
MARLPIT LANE
LEYS ROAD
BACK LANE
HAVERCROFT LANE
Valley Plantation
ASH GROVE
ELM CL
BEECH CRESCENT
DENBY RD
SOTHERON CROFT
PARK CLOSE
DENBY PARK AVE
PHILIPS LANE
DENBY CREST
MILL HILL CLOSE
School
WENTWORTH PARK RISE
HILL CROFT CLOSE
Church
Post Office
Darrington
CHURCH LANE
ESTCOURT ROAD
ORCHARD VIEW
NEW ROW COTTAGES
GREENROYD COURT
THORNTREE CLOSE
MILNER'S LANE
MANOR PARK
MANOR PARK RISE
ESTCOURT DRIVE
OLD GREAT NORTH ROAD
FAIRWAYS COURT
VALLEY ROAD
NORTH LODGE LANE
BANK WOOD ROAD
WESTFIELD LANE
WEST PARK TERRACE
WEST PARK DRIVE

TRADE REFUSE COLLECTION
ALL WHEELED CONTAINERS & DUSTBINS

City of Wakefield Metropolitan District Council — Public Services Department

Telephone 01977 722000

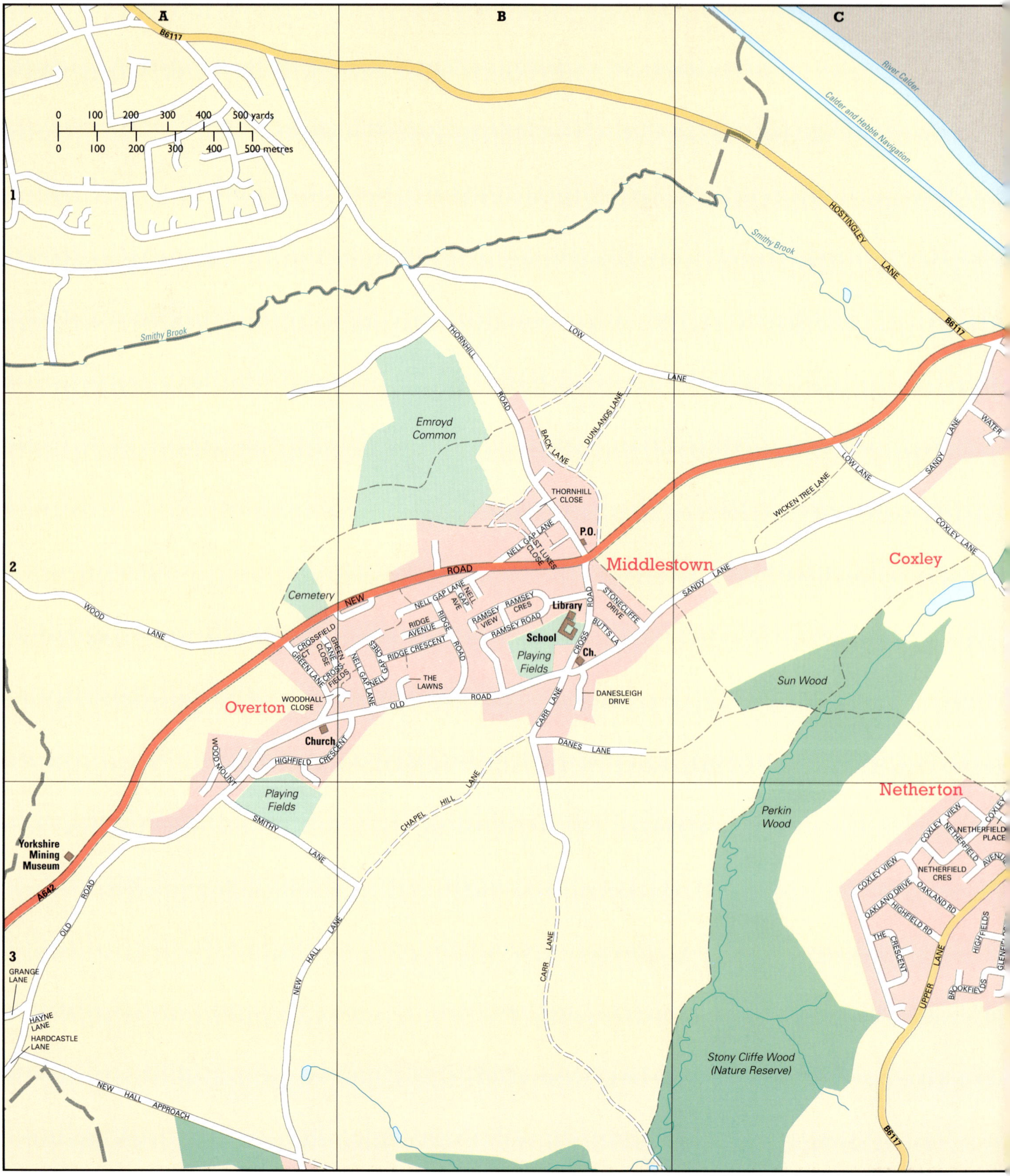

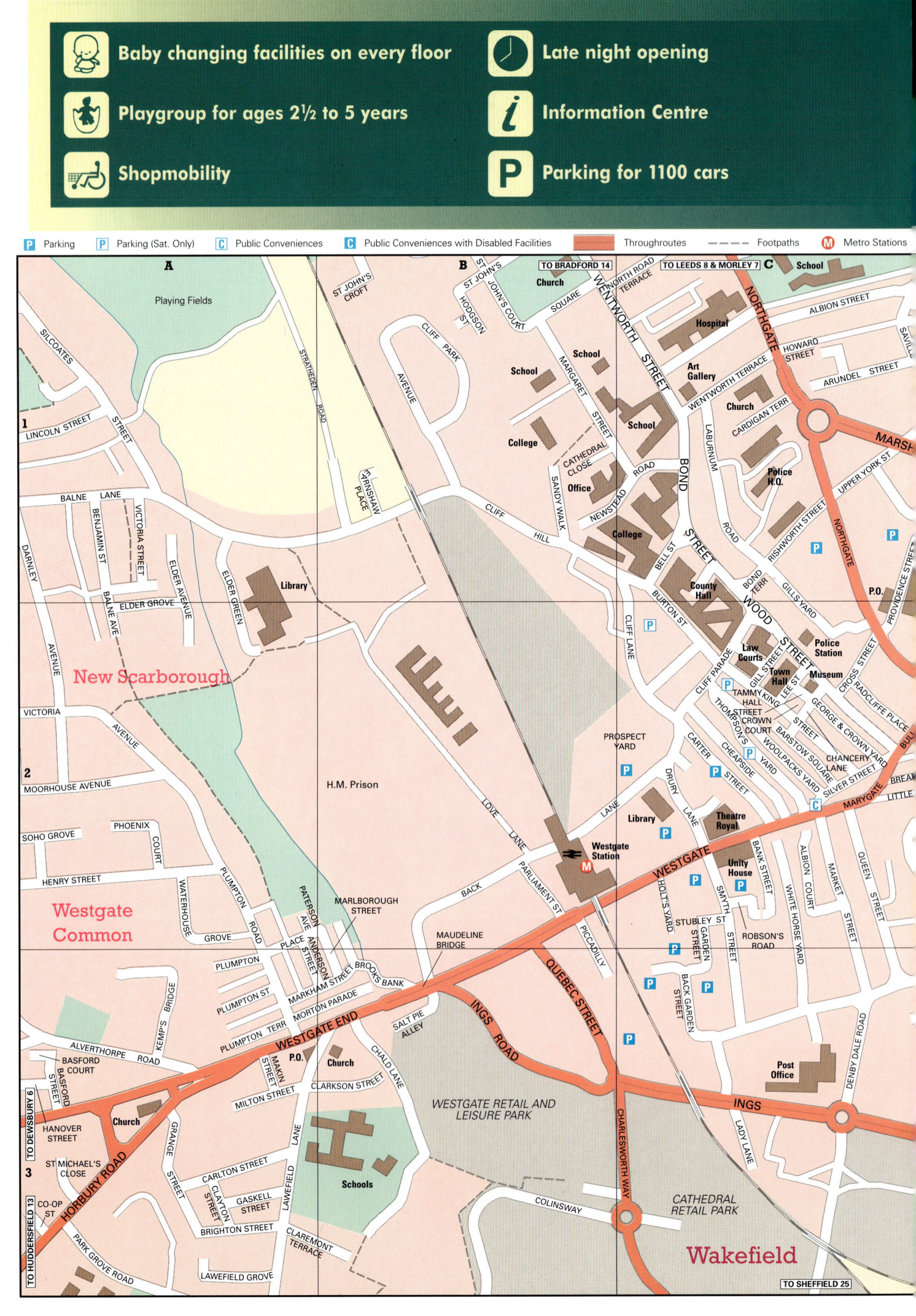

The Ridings Shopping Centre WAKEFIELD

Telephone 01924 787787

"...Impressive Choice, Unbeatable Service and Superb Facilities for all the Family"

get on board

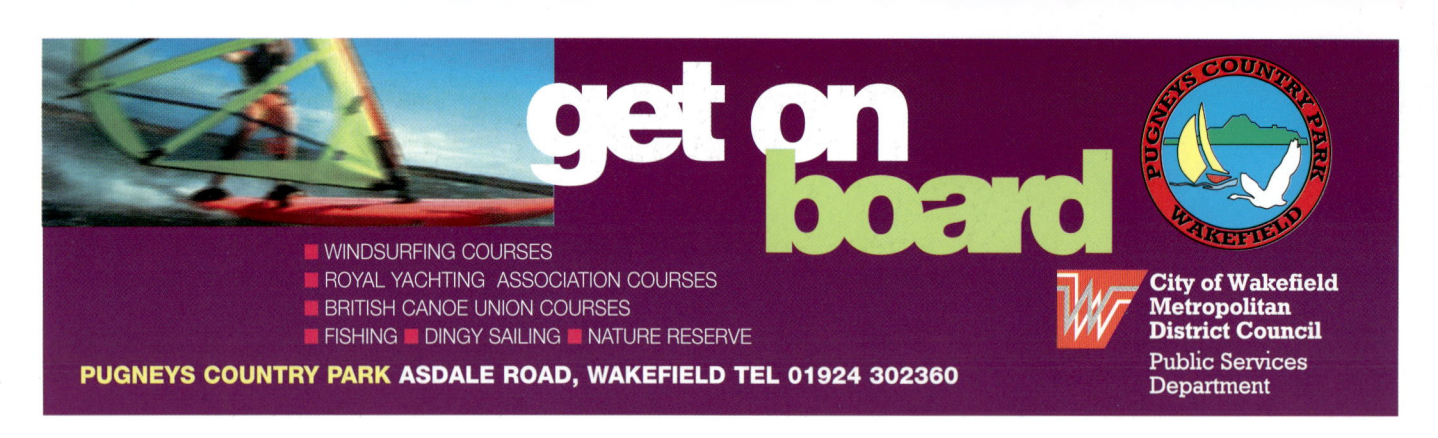

- WINDSURFING COURSES
- ROYAL YACHTING ASSOCIATION COURSES
- BRITISH CANOE UNION COURSES
- FISHING ■ DINGY SAILING ■ NATURE RESERVE

PUGNEYS COUNTRY PARK ASDALE ROAD, WAKEFIELD TEL 01924 302360

Pugneys Country Park — Wakefield

City of Wakefield Metropolitan District Council
Public Services Department

highly strung?

Sweat it out in the sauna
and cool off afterwards in the leisure pool

LIGHTWAVES LEISURE CENTRE MARSH WAY, WAKEFIELD TEL: 01924 302330

Light waves LEISURE CENTRE

City of Wakefield Metropolitan District Council
Public Services Department

Panasonic
The State of the Art

Panasonic (UK) Ltd., Kenmore Road, Wakefield 41 Business Park, Wakefield WF2 0XE

Cash when you need it most

Looking after your health can be costly. We can help by offering generous cash payments on a wide range of benefits including...

- UP TO **£50** TOWARDS A PAIR OF GLASSES
- UP TO **£50** TOWARDS YOUR DENTAL BILLS
- WE PAY YOU **£18** PER NIGHT* FOR A STAY IN HOSPITAL *After the first night

FOR ONLY 95p PER WEEK Group and individual membership available

PHB
PREMIER HEALTH BENEFITS
Supporting the NHS since 1948

For further information please telephone
Wakefield 01924 373500

Wakefield and District Hospitals Contributory Scheme Ltd. Registered Charity No.226121. Income realised by the charity's investments is devoted to improving health care and health related facilities.

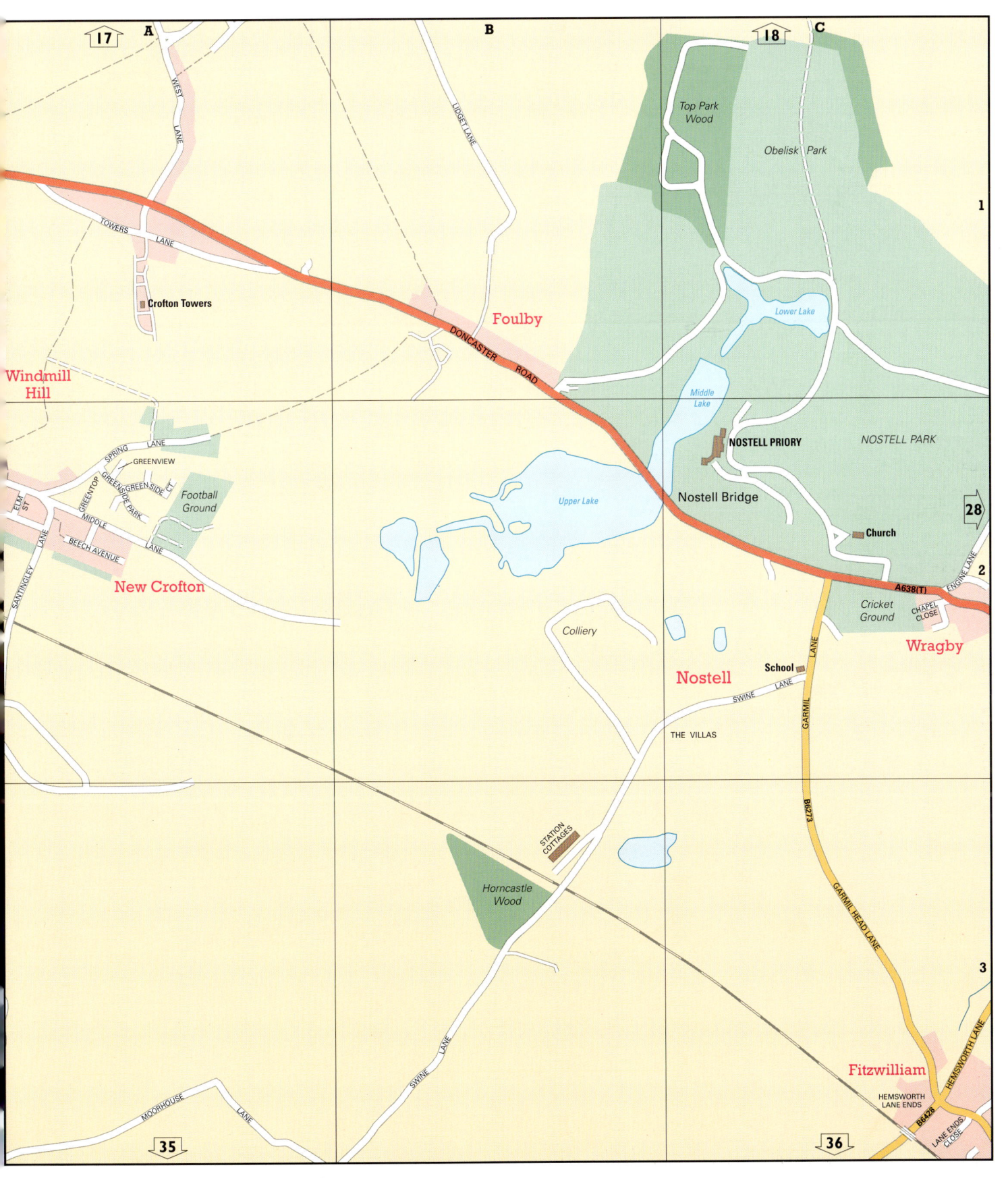

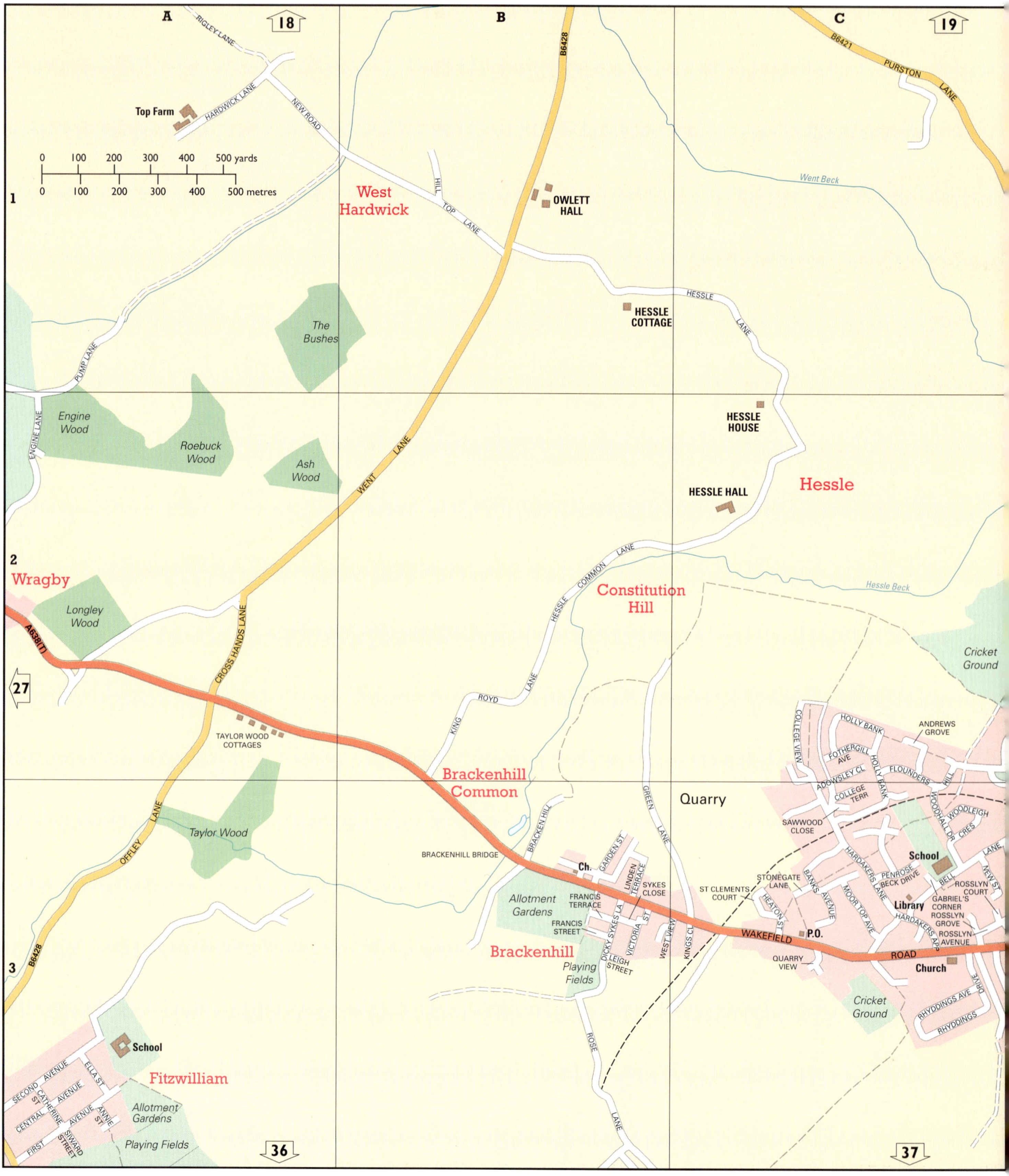
A
B
C
18
19
27
36
37
1
2
3
0 100 200 300 400 500 yards
0 100 200 300 400 500 metres
RIGLEY LANE
Top Farm
HARDWICK LANE
NEW ROAD
B6428
B6421
PURSTON LANE
West Hardwick
HILL
TOP LANE
OWLETT HALL
Went Beck
HESSLE LANE
HESSLE COTTAGE
The Bushes
PUMP LANE
Engine Wood
ENGINE LANE
Roebuck Wood
Ash Wood
WENT LANE
HESSLE HOUSE
HESSLE HALL
Hessle
HESSLE COMMON LANE
Constitution Hill
Hessle Beck
Wragby
Longley Wood
A638(T)
CROSS HANDS LANE
Cricket Ground
KING ROYD LANE
TAYLOR WOOD COTTAGES
COLLEGE VIEW
HOLLY BANK
ANDREWS GROVE
FOTHERGILL AVE
ADOWSLEY CL
COLLEGE TERR
FLOUNDERS HILL
WOODLEIGH CRES
Brackenhill Common
Quarry
GREEN LANE
SAWWOOD CLOSE
Taylor Wood
OFFLEY LANE
BRACKEN HILL
BRACKENHILL BRIDGE
Ch.
GARDEN ST
LINDEN TERRACE
SYKES CLOSE
School
PENROSE BECK DRIVE
ROSSLYN COURT
Allotment Gardens
FRANCIS TERRACE
FRANCIS STREET
DICKY SYKES LA
VICTORIA ST
WEST VIEW
KINGS CL
ST CLEMENTS COURT
STONEGATE LANE
HEATON ST
BANKS AVENUE
MOOR TOP AVE
HARDAKERS LANE
Library
GABRIEL'S CORNER
ROSSLYN GROVE
ROSSLYN AVENUE
HARDAKERS APP
P.O.
WAKEFIELD ROAD
Church
Brackenhill
LEIGH STREET
Playing Fields
QUARRY VIEW
Cricket Ground
RHYDDINGS AVE
RHYDDINGS
DRIVE
ROSE LANE
School
Fitzwilliam
SECOND AVENUE
ELLA ST
CATHERINE ST
CENTRAL AVENUE
AVENUE
ANNIE ST
FIRST
SEWARD STREET
Allotment Gardens
Playing Fields

Gold is the colour for special occasions

Anniversary, Birthday or New Arrival? To celebrate your special event in style tel 01924 826128

Britannia Business Centre

INDUSTRIAL, COMMERCIAL & DOMESTIC CLEANING

House & Factory Clearances
Builder's Clean
Hazardous & Contaminated Work

WASTE REMOVAL SERVICES

Industrial, Commercial & Domestic Waste
Drug-related items, Sharps & Hazardous Waste

BUILDING PRESERVATION SERVICES

Dry and Wet Rot & Timber Infestation Treatment
Mould Growth Eradication
Cellar Tanking

HOUSEHOLD & COMMERCIAL SERVICES

Property Boarding & Securing
Building, Plastering & Joinery
Fire Damage & Flood Repairs
Plumbing & Electrical
Painting & Decorating
French Polishing
Pest & Insect Control
Furniture Re-upholstery
Specialist Laundry & Dry Cleaning

Britannia House
Pildacre Lane • Ossett • Wakefield • WF5 8HN
Telephone: 01924 279988 • Fax: 01924 267788 • Mobile nos: 0850 310977 / 0585 255571
e-mail: Britannia4Business@compuserve.com

Contractors to Local Authorities, Solicitors, Estate Agents and Insurance Companies

A Complete Service

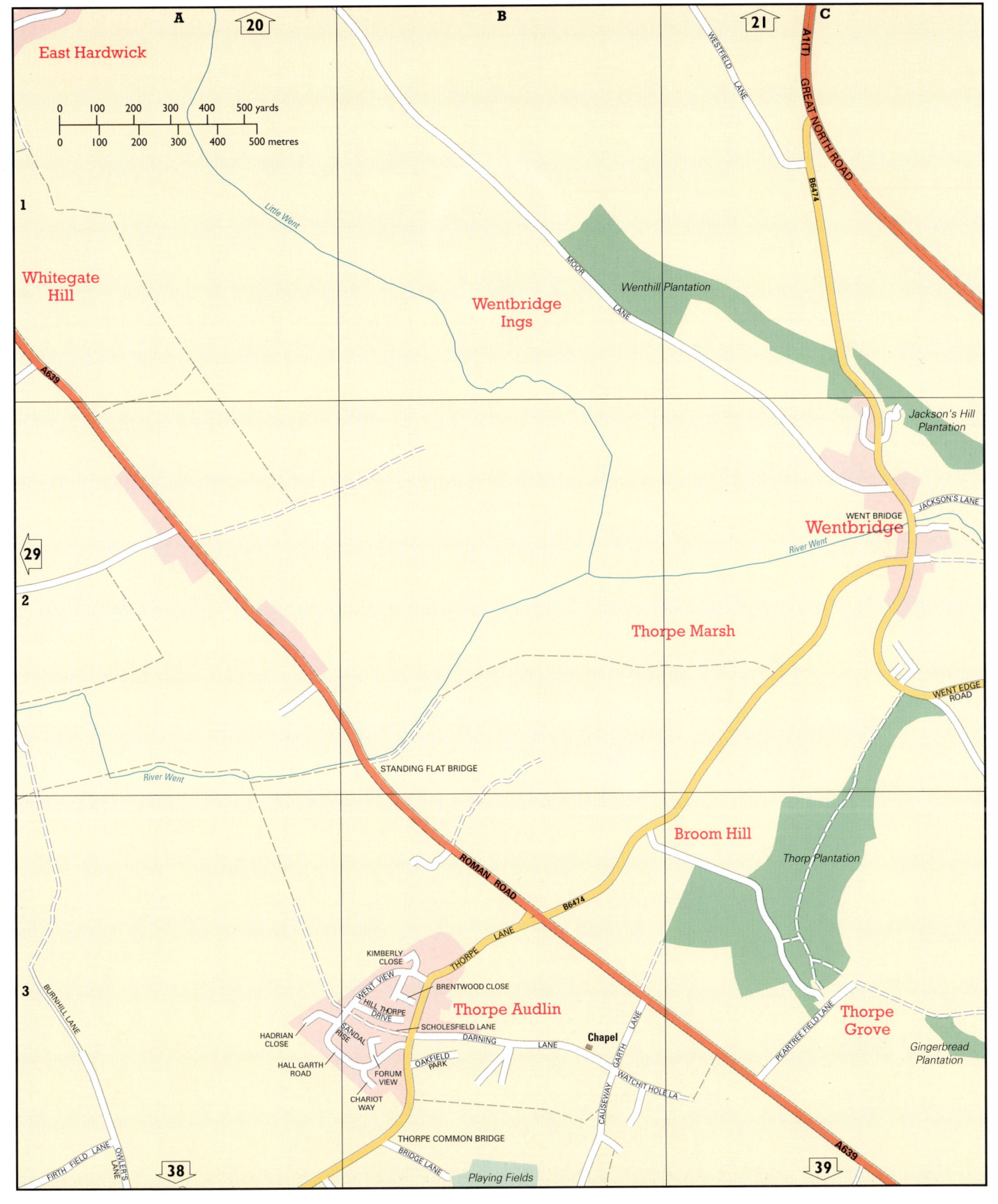

from concept to design through to high quality laser and offset litho printing

Design and Print Services
Cliff Lane, Wakefield WF1 2TN
Tel **01924 305776** Fax 01924 305782

City of Wakefield Metropolitan District Council

Map

East Hardwick
Whitegate Hill
Wentbridge Ings
Wenthill Plantation
Jackson's Hill Plantation
Wentbridge
Thorpe Marsh
Broom Hill
Thorp Plantation
Thorpe Audlin
Thorpe Grove
Gingerbread Plantation

Roads and features: A639, A1(T) Great North Road, B6474, Westfield Lane, Moor Lane, Jackson's Lane, Went Bridge, River Went, Went Edge Road, Standing Flat Bridge, Roman Road, Thorpe Lane, Kimberly Close, Went View, Hill Thorpe Drive, Brentwood Close, Scholesfield Lane, Darning Lane, Chapel, Garth Lane, Peartree Field Lane, Hadrian Close, Sandal Rise, Oakfield Park, Watchit Hole La, Causeway, Hall Garth Road, Forum View, Chariot Way, Burnhill Lane, Firth Field Lane, Owler's Lane, Thorpe Common Bridge, Bridge Lane, Playing Fields, Little Went

30

Going by MetroCard saves money like magic!

IT'S CHEAPER BY CARD

ⓘ METRO TRAVEL INFORMATION – PHONE 0113 245 7676

Ⓜ METRO HERE TO GET YOU THERE

"Waiter"

Come and have a relaxing time at Restaurant *Michel Laurens*

Traditional Menus

Lunch from £3.90
3 courses • 12noon to 2pm • Tuesday - Friday

Dinner from £9.50
4 courses • 5.30 to 9.00pm • Wed - Friday

For more information contact Restaurant *Michel Laurens*.
Tel. 01924 789505
Wakefield College, Margaret Street, Wakefield, West Yorkshire. WF1 2DH.

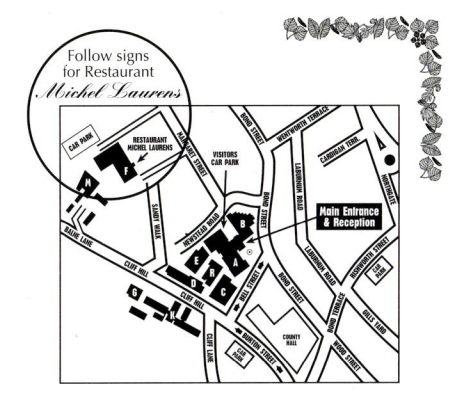

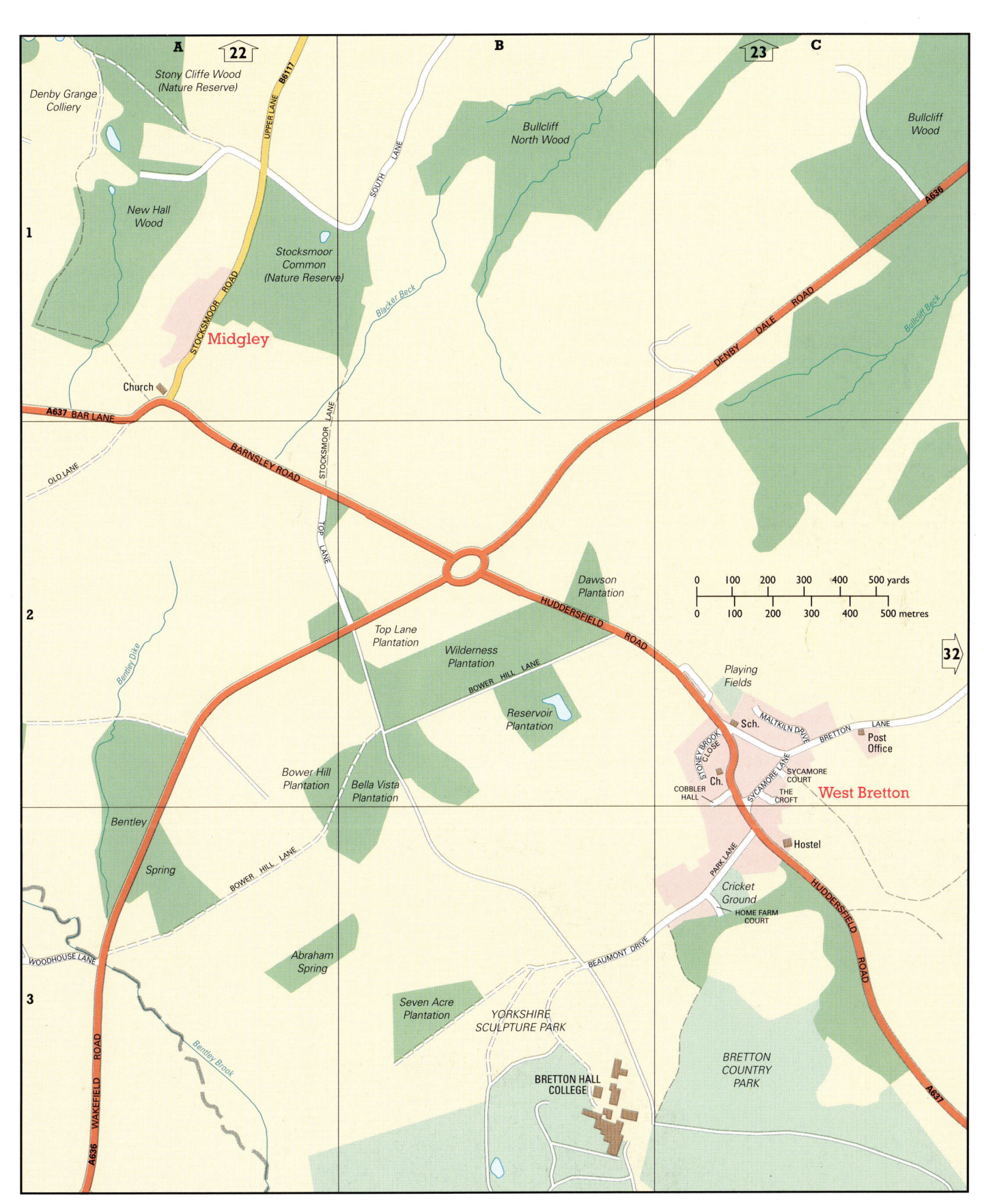

Follow signs for Restaurant *Michel Laurens*

HODSONS
ESTATE · AGENTS

Wakefield's Leading Independent Estate Agent

Tel: 01924 200544

THEATRE ROYAL & OPERA HOUSE

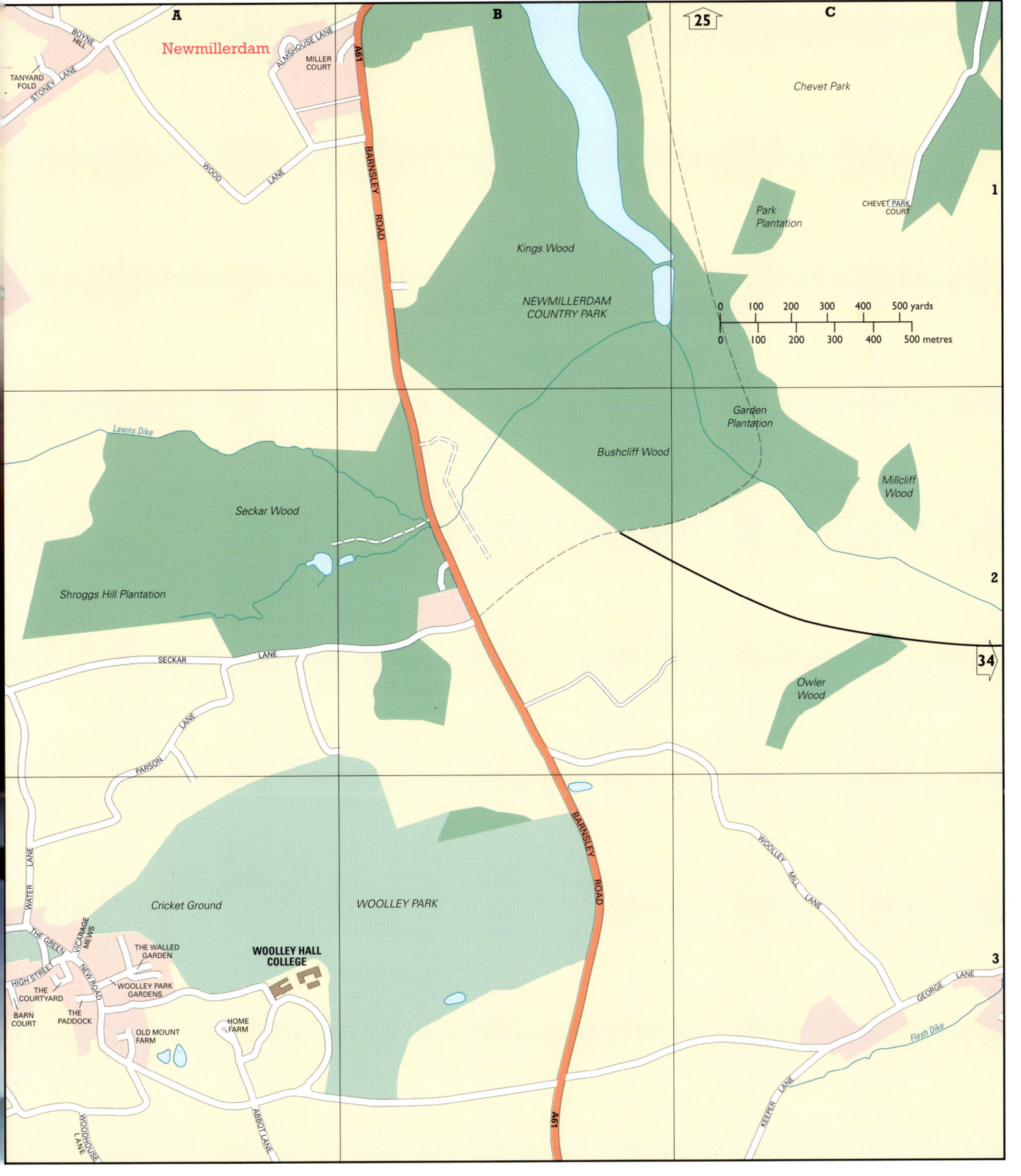

music · DRAMA · DANCE · comedy

Drury Lane, Wakefield WF1 2TE
Box Office **01924 211311**
Minicom 01924 215522
e.mail WKFIELD-THEATRE@geo2.poptel.org.uk

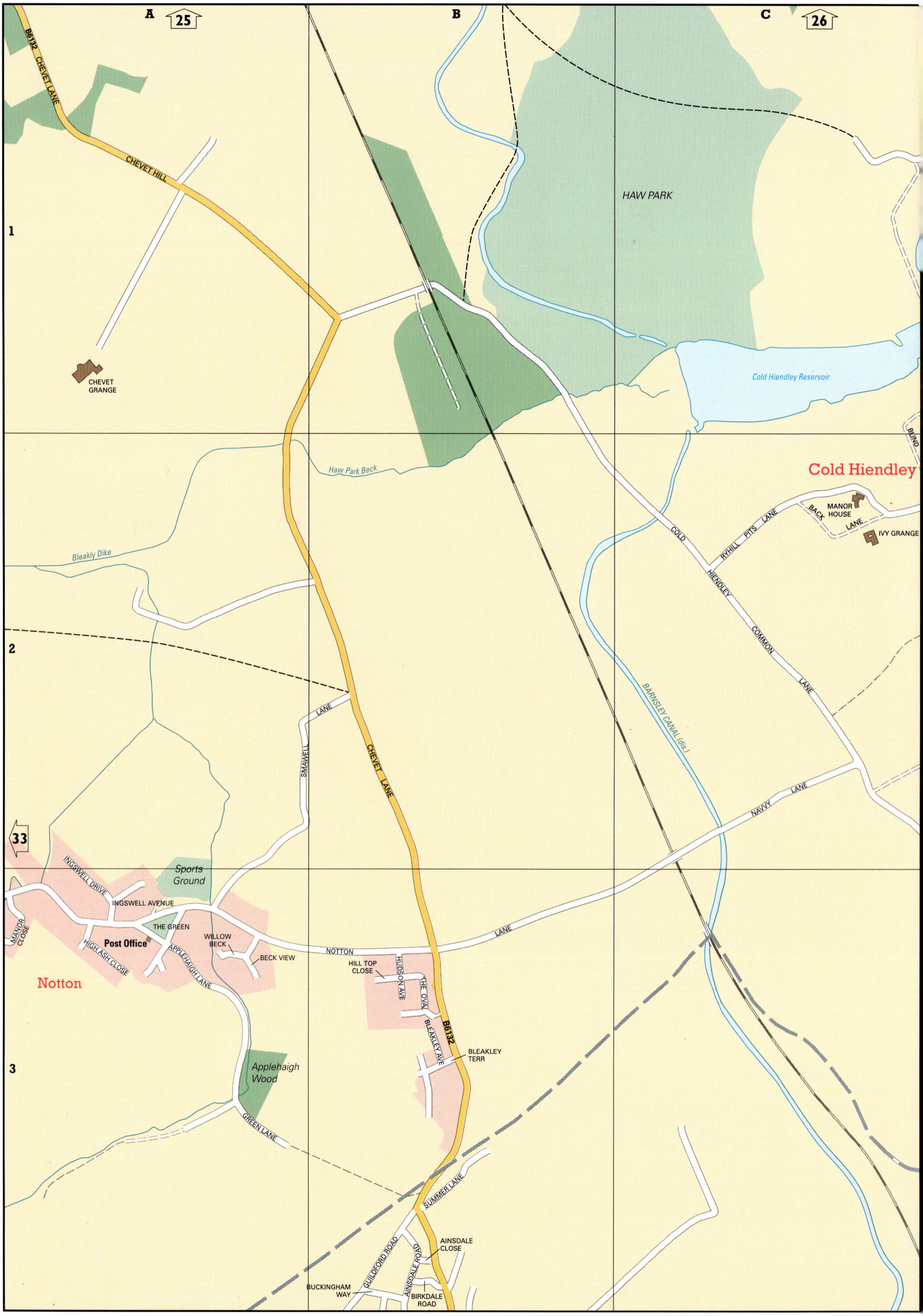
A
25
B
C
26
1
2
3
33
B6132 CHEVET LANE
CHEVET HILL
CHEVET GRANGE
HAW PARK
Cold Hiendley Reservoir
Cold Hiendley
MANOR HOUSE
BACK LANE
IVY GRANGE
RYHILL PITS LANE
COLD HIENDLEY COMMON LANE
BLIND
Haw Park Beck
Bleakly Dike
BARNSLEY CANAL (dis)
SMAWELL LANE
CHEVET LANE
NAVVY LANE
NOTTON LANE
Sports Ground
INGSWELL DRIVE
INGSWELL AVENUE
THE GREEN
MANOR CLOSE
Post Office
HIGH ASH CLOSE
APPLEHAIGH LANE
WILLOW BECK
BECK VIEW
Notton
HILL TOP CLOSE
HUDSON AVE
THE OVAL
BLEAKLEY AVE
B6132
BLEAKLEY TERR
Applehaigh Wood
GREEN LANE
SUMMER LANE
AINSDALE CLOSE
GUILDFORD ROAD
AINSDALE ROAD
BUCKINGHAM WAY
BIRKDALE ROAD

A
B
C
27
36
1
2
3
0 100 200 300 400 500 yards
0 100 200 300 400 500 metres
Wintersett Reservoir
Ryhill Pitts
Ryhill
Havercroft
South Hiendley
HAW PARK LANE
FERRY TOP LANE
LONG DAM LANE
NOSTELL LANE
COMMON ING LANE
RYHILL PITS LANE
STATION ROAD
HOOTON CRESCENT
WESTFIELD CRESCENT
SUNNY BANK
LAFFLANDS LANE
CHAPEL ST
ST ANNE'S STREET
SCHOOL LANE
CEMETERY ROAD
GEORGE STREET
CHURCH FIELDS
LAKESIDE ESTATE
BRUNSWICK
QUARRY MOUNT TERRACE
GARDEN LANE
MILL LANE
TOP ORCHARD
GREENSIDE
MULBERRY PLACE
MULBERRY AVENUE
COW LANE
EASTMOUNT
BRIER LANE
JUBILEE COTTAGES
HENRY AVENUE
HOPE ST
HAVERCROFT GREEN
TEN LANDS LANE
CHURCH LANE
ELLIS LAITHE FOLD
HALL FIELD LANE
LUND HILL LANE
B6428
SLACK LANE
RAVEN LANE
HIGH WELL HILL LANE
HIGH WELL LA
WESTOFF LANE
TUP LANE
FARFIELD LANE
ST JAMES COURT
MEADOW BANK
HAVERDALE ROAD
HARDIE ROAD
HILL CREST
ATTLEE AVENUE
REGINA CRESCENT
CRESCENT ROAD
SOUTH STREET
WEST STREET
EAST STREET
CHURCH VIEW
CHURCH CLOSE
MADELEY
LODGES CLOSE
RYECROFT AVE
GREENACRE WALK
INGS ROAD
INGS CLOSE
HORNCASTLE VIEW
ST GEORGES COURT
UPPER HATFIELD PLACE
HATFIELD PL
HIGHFIELDS
BROOKLANDS CRESCENT
ING LANE
COMMON
TUN LANE
BRAEMAR RISE
BRAEMAR CROFT
WHITE CROSS GARDENS
GEORGE STREET
KIRKGATE LA
NEW ST
MANOR CROFT
ORCHARD DRIVE
MAIN STREET
CHESTNUT DRIVE
Allotment Gardens
Cemetery
Sports Ground
Playing Fields
Ch.
Chapel
Sch.
Church
Hall
Library
School
P.O.

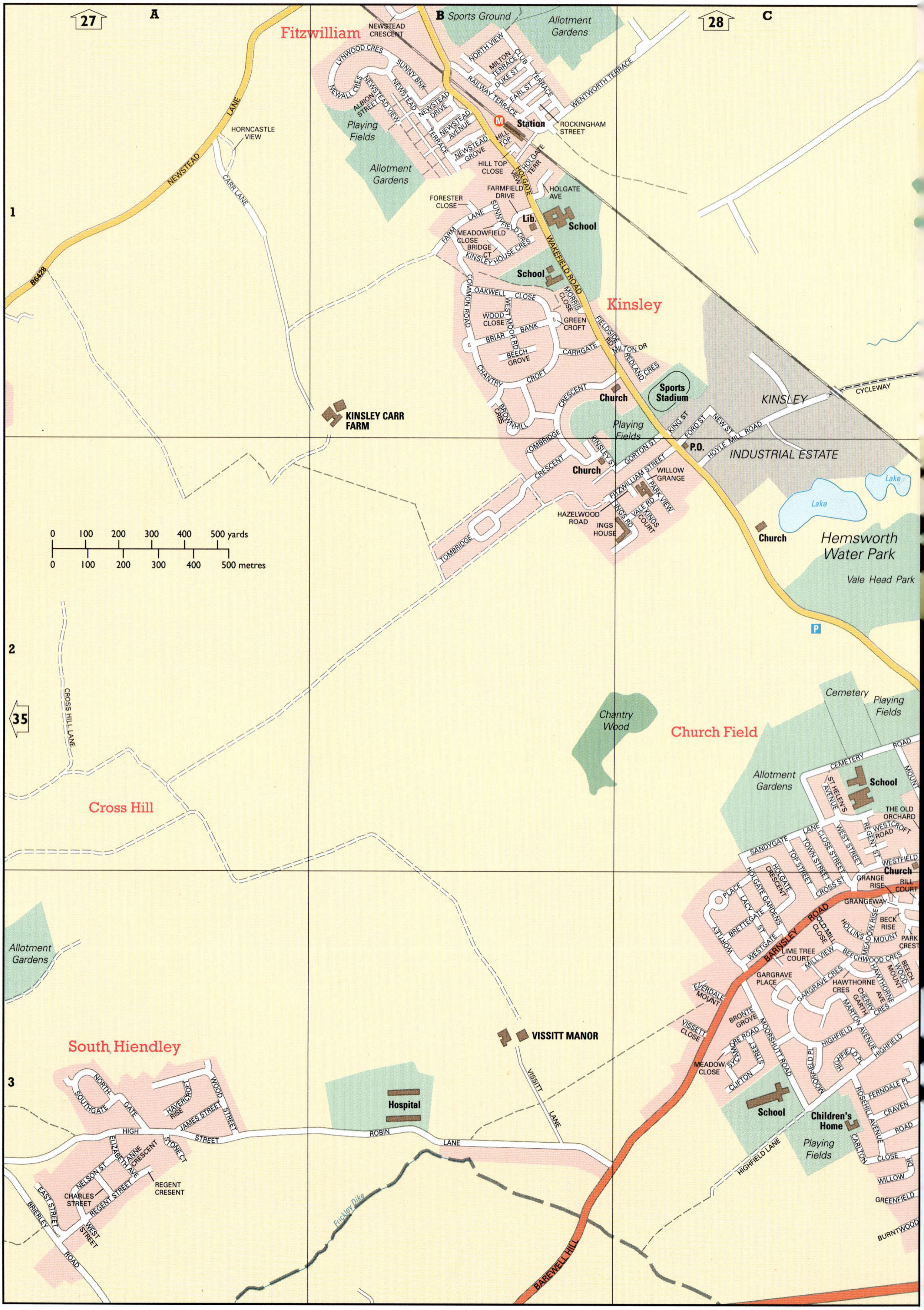

A
B
C
29
SCHOLEY'S BRIDGE
Shepherd's Hill
DOUNCASTER ROAD
ROSE LANE
A628
Bingley Spring Wood
CYCLEWAY
HOYLE MILL ROAD
Hoyle Mill Dam
Lakeside View
Hagg Wood
HOYLE MILL ROAD
PONTEFRACT ROAD
Badsworth Common
A638
1
38
Anthony's Quarry Wood
The Snipery
Marsh Whin Covert
Hemsworth Marsh
Marsh Plantation
ROYD MOOR LANE
2
SPRINGVALE RISE
WOODLANDS
SUSSEX CLOSE
HEREFORD CLOSE
DORSET CLOSE
NORTH WALK
CRES
STATION ROAD
Butcher Wood
Playing Fields
WAKEFIELD ROAD
LODGE ST
CENTRE STREET
HOLLY STREET
BUTCHER HILL
Offices
School
College
RECTORY GARTH
MAYFAIR PLACE
School
WOOD MOOR RD
EAST DALE CL
MARSH LEA GROVE
Ch.
LOWFIELD ROAD
ALBANY TERRACE
CROSS HILL
Bollinger Wood
PEAR TREE LANE
CHURCH CLOSE
School
EATON PLACE
LOWFIELD CRES
CHILTERN COURT
Lib.
COTTAM CROFT
LEYBROOK CROFT
CHEVIOT CLOSE
PENNINE WAY
COTSWOLD CLOSE
MORVERN MEADOWS
P.O.
Bus Station
PLIMSOLL STREET
Police
SPRINGSTONE AVENUE
RIDGESTONE AVENUE
VALESTONE AVENUE
BROOKSIDE
ELM ROAD
RINGWOOD WAY
BANK ST
Green Hill
MARKET STREET
Hemsworth
BELMONT CRES
BREDON CLOSE
Wheat Royds
CHEVIOT DRIVE
LITTLE HEMSWORTH
Offices
LILLEY ST
Allotment Gardens
Church
BULLENSHAW ROAD
HIGH ST
GROVE TERRACE
GROVE LEA CLOSE
GROVE PL
GROVE AVENUE
BAYLEE STREET
Ch.
GROVE LANE
BULLENSHAW VILLAS
School
HAMEL RISE
KING EDWARD ST
Allotment Gardens
BUSH ST
JUNCTION ST
PONTEFRACT TERRACE
UNION ST
THOMAS ST
VICTORIA STREET
3
SPRINGFIELD AVENUE
EASTGATE
OAK TREE GR
ELIZABETH COURT
Hospital
SOUTH STREET
KIRKBY ROAD
HAGUE TERRACE
DRIVE
Common End
WINDSOR ROAD
DALE VIEW
PENLINGTON CLOSE
ROAD
YORK ST
ASHFIELD
THORNTON CLOSE
MOOR TOP DRIVE
OAKWOOD
HILMIAN WAY
JUBILEE CLOSE
CHESTNUT GROVE
KIRKBYGATE LANE
RIDDINGS CLOSE
SOUTHMOOR ROAD
HAGUE CRESCENT
WHIN CLOSE
KIRKBYGATE
NOR WOOD ROAD
MEADOW CROFT
BANK
HEMSWORTH ROAD
41
B6273
40
B6422
Hague Plantation

Rogerthorpe Manor Country Hotel

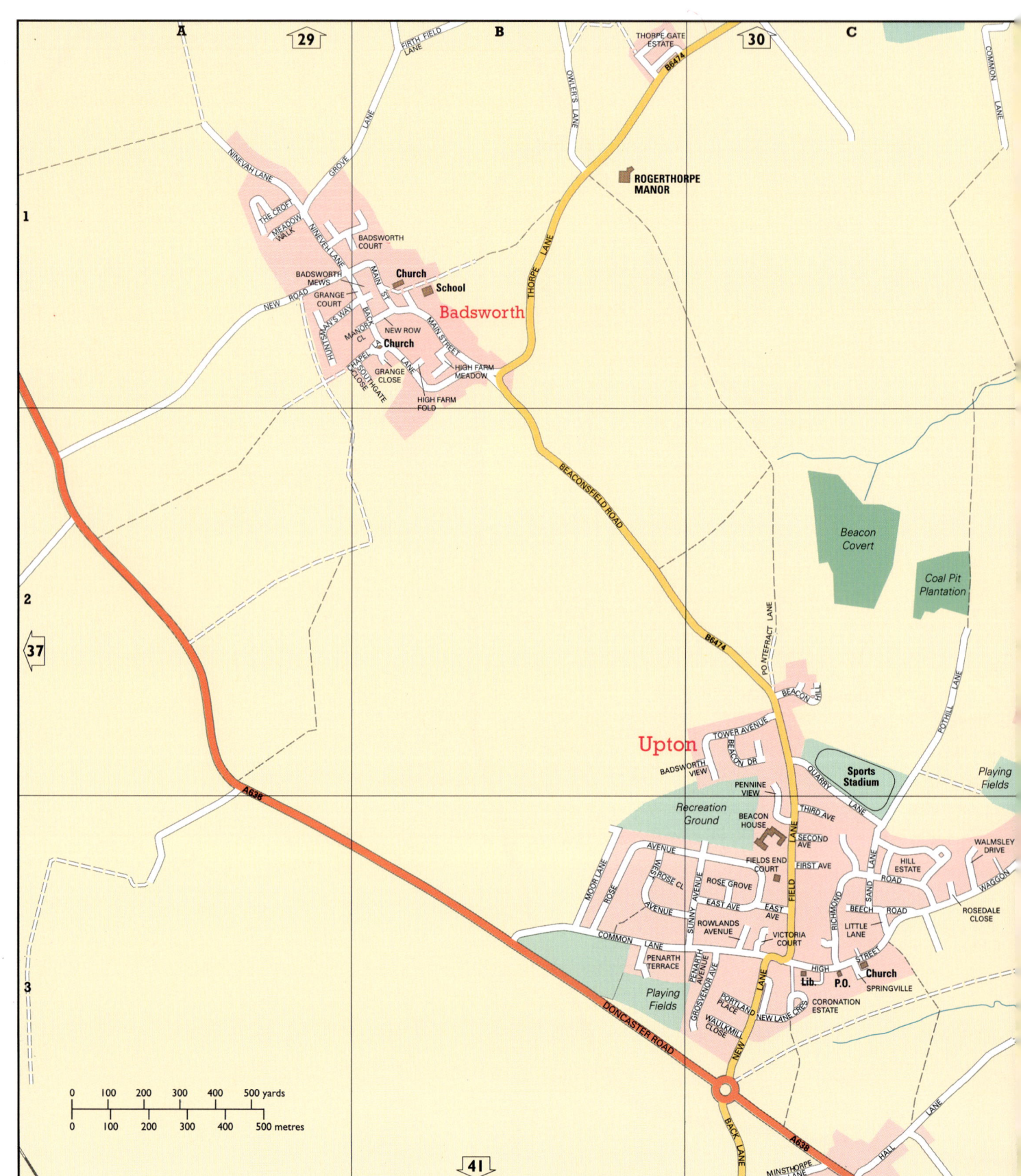

Thorpe Lane
Badsworth
Pontefract WF9 1AB

Facsimile 01977 645704

English Tourist Board COMMENDED

- Conferences
- Weddings (*On-site Licence*)
- Dinners
- Accommodation
- Murder Mystery Nights

TELEPHONE **01977 643839**

To put **your** organisation on the **map**....
Telephone **01924 305290**.

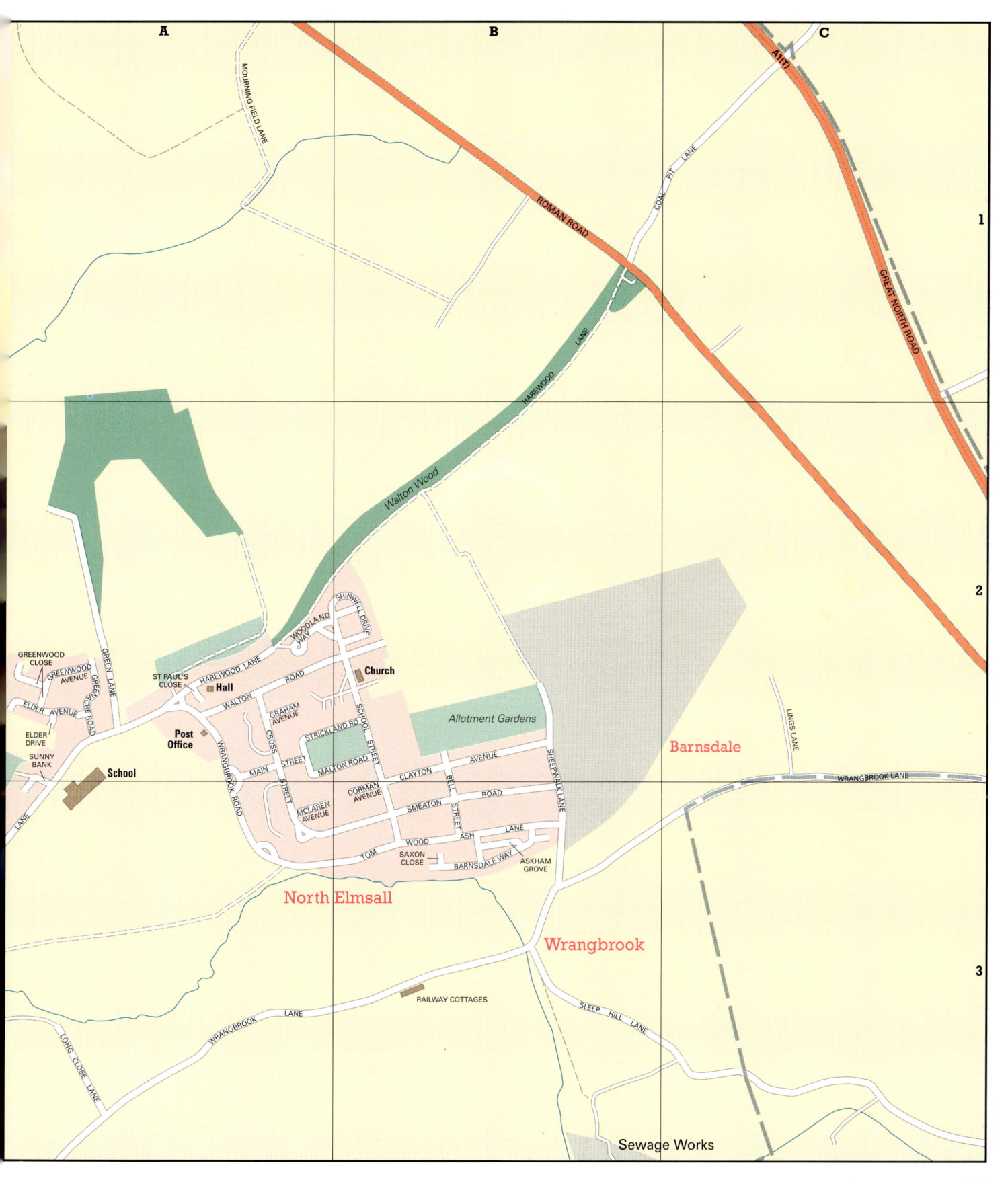

WAKEFIELD DISTRICT STREET ATLAS

North Elmsall
Barnsdale
Wrangbrook

39

Cash when you need it most

Looking after your health can be costly. We can help by offering generous cash payments on a wide range of benefits including...

UP TO £50 TOWARDS A PAIR OF GLASSES

UP TO £50 TOWARDS YOUR DENTAL BILLS

WE PAY YOU £18 PER NIGHT* FOR A STAY IN HOSPITAL
*After the first night

FOR ONLY 95p PER WEEK
Group and individual membership available

PHB
PREMIER HEALTH BENEFITS
Supporting the NHS since 1948

For further information please telephone
Wakefield 01924 373500

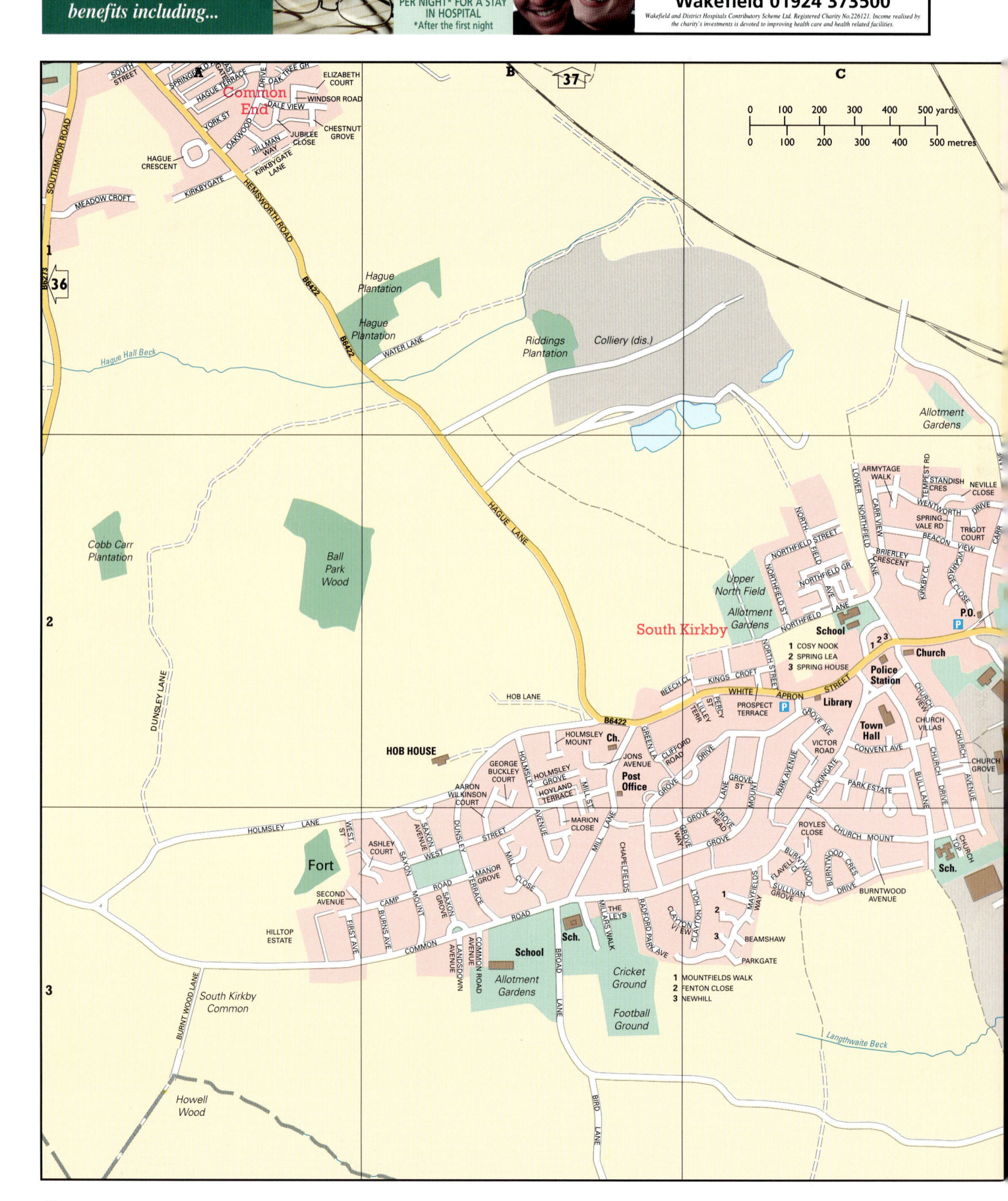

Wakefield and District Hospitals Contributory Scheme Ltd. Registered Charity No.226121. Income realised by the charity's investments is devoted to improving health care and health related facilities.

over 1000 stalls and market shops

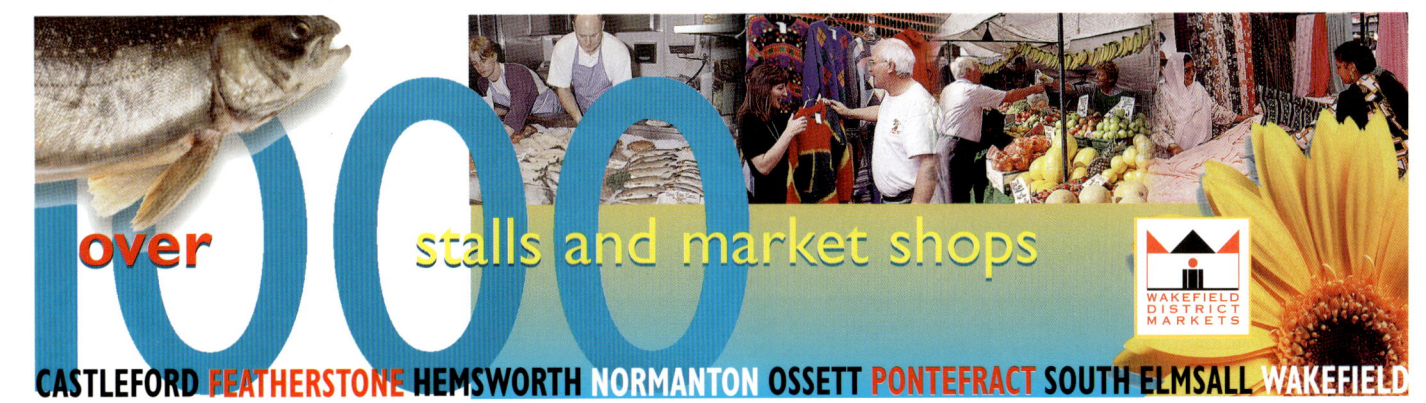

WAKEFIELD DISTRICT MARKETS

CASTLEFORD **FEATHERSTONE** HEMSWORTH NORMANTON OSSETT **PONTEFRACT** SOUTH ELMSALL WAKEFIELD

Moorthorpe / South Elmsall

41

STREET INDEX

The street index is in alphabetical order. Map Page numbers are shown in **bold** followed by the grid reference. **T/C** refers to the Town Centre Map in the middle of this Guide.

A

Street	Page	Grid
Aaron Wilkinson Court	40	B3
Abbot Lane	33	A3
Abbots Close	10	A3
Abbott Terrace	15	C3
Aberfield Drive	24	A3
Aberford Road	5	C3/6 A1
Acacia Avenue (South Elmsall)	41	C1
Acacia Close (Ferrybridge)	3	A2
Acacia Drive (Ferrybridge)	3	A2
Acacia Green	10	B3
Acacia Walk	11	B2
Ackton Close	8	B3
Ackton Hall Cottages	8	B3
Ackton Hall Crescent	8	B3
Ackton Lane	8	B3
Ackton Pasture Lane	1	B3
Ackworth Bridle Road	29	C2
Ackworth Carr Bridge	29	A2
Ackworth House Close	29	A2
Ackworth Road (Featherstone)	19	A3
Ackworth Road (Pontefract)	20	A2
Acme Terrace	15	C3
Acute Terrace	14	C2
Addingford Close	23	B1
Addingford Drive	23	B1
Addingford Lane	23	B1
Addison Avenue	7	C3
Addison Court	14	B3
Addy Crescent	41	B2
Adowsley Close	28	C2
Adwick Grove	24	C3
Adwick Terrace	10	B2
Agbrigg Grove	25	B1
Agbrigg Road	15	C3/25 B1
Agincourt Drive	6	C2
Ainsdale Close	34	B3
Ainsdale Road	34	B3
Aire Street (Castleford)	2	A2
Aire Street (Knottingley)	11	C1
Aire Terrace	1	C1
Aire View	11	B1
Aire Walk	11	C1
Airedale Drive	3	A1
Airedale Heights	14	A2
Airedale Road	2	C2
Aketon Drive	1	C1
Aketon Road	1	C2
Albany Court	20	A1
Albany Crescent	41	B2
Albany Place	41	B2
Albany Street	41	B2
Albany Terrace	37	A2
Albert Street (Featherstone)	19	A2
Albert Street (Normanton)	7	C2
Albion Court	15	B1
Albion Court	T/C	C2
Albion Croft	13	B2
Albion Place	41	B2
Albion Square	14	C1
Albion Street (Castleford)	1	C2
Albion Street (Fitzwilliam)	36	B1
Albion Street (Wakefield)	15	B1
Albion Street	T/C	C1
Alden Crescent	19	C1
Alder Avenue	15	A1
Alder Grove	17	B1
Alexander Crescent	19	A1
Alexander Road	19	A1
Alexandra Drive	17	B1
All Saints View	10	B3
Allan Haigh Close	14	B1
Allison Street	18	C2
Allison Terrace	4	A3
Allott Close	41	B2
Almond Close	41	C1
Almshouse Lane (Newmillerdam)	33	A1
Almshouse Lane (Pledwick)	24	C3
Almshouse Lane (Wakefield)	15	B2
Almshouse Lane	T/C	D2
Almshouses	24	C3
Altinkool Street	15	C3
Altofts Hall Road	7	A2
Altofts Lane	7	C1
Altofts Lodge Drive	7	A2
Altofts Road	7	B2
Alverthorpe Road	T/C	A3
Alverthorpe Road	14	C1
Ambler Street	2	A2
Ambleside Drive	25	C2
Ambleside Road	3	A1
Anaheim Drive	5	B1
Andersen Court	3	A3
Anderson Street (Pontefract)	9	C3
Anderton Street (Wakefield)	15	C3
Anderson Street	T/C	A3
Andrew Crescent	5	A1
Andrew Street (Featherstone)	18	C2
Andrew Street	15	A1
Andrews Grove	28	C2
Anne Crescent	36	A3
Annie Street (Fitzwilliam)	28	A3
Annie Street (Outwood)	5	A2
Anston Drive	41	B1
Apple Tree Close	19	C1
Apple Tree Road	19	A3
Applegarth	25	B2
Applehaigh Lane	34	A3
Appleshaw Crescent	4	C2
Archer Street	1	C2
Arden Court	23	B1
Argyle Road	11	A1
Argyle Street	15	C3
Argyll Avenue	19	C1
Arlington Grove	2	B2
Arlington Street	5	A3
Armitage Road	4	B3
Armitage Street	1	C1
Armstrong Close	7	A2
Armstrong Terrace	19	C1
Armytage Walk	40	C2
Arncliff Road	15	C1
Arncliffe Drive	11	A1
Arncliffe Road	16	A1
Arnside Close	3	A2
Arnside Crescent	3	A2
Arthur Street	15	C3
Arundel Street	15	B1
Arundel Street	T/C	C1
Asdale Road	24	C2
Ash Close	13	B2
Ash Crescent	6	A2
Ash Green	10	B3
Ash Grove (Darrington)	21	A2
Ash Grove (South Elmsall)	41	B1
Ash Grove (Wakefield)	5	C3
Ash Lea	5	C2
Ash Street (New Crofton)	26	C2
Ash Street (Wakefield)	6	A2
Ash Tree Gardens	7	A2
Ashbourne Drive	20	A2
Ashbrook Close	13	B2
Ashbury Chase	5	A1
Ashcombe Drive	11	C2
Ashcroft Avenue	18	C3
Ashdale	25	B1
Ashdene Avenue	26	C1
Ashdene Crescent	26	C1
Ashdene Drive	26	C1
Ashdene Garth	26	C1
Ashdene Grove	10	C2
Ashdene Approach	26	B1
Ashdown Road	15	C3
Ashfield Road	37	A3
Ashfield Street	7	B2
Ashgap Lane	7	B2
Ashlar Grove	2	B2
Ashlea Court	24	C3
Ashleigh Avenue (Pontefract)	20	A1
Ashleigh Avenue (Wakefield)	14	C2
Ashleigh Gardens	13	A1
Ashley Close	4	C3
Ashley Court	40	B3
Ashmore Drive	13	A1
Ashton Court	24	C3
Ashton Road	2	A2
Ashton Street	2	A2
Ashwood Grove	23	C1
Ashwood Villas	19	C1
Askam Avenue	3	C3
Askham Grove	39	A3
Askham Road	3	A1
Aspen Close	15	A1
Ass Hill	10	B3
Assembly Street	7	B3
Aston Court	14	A2
Athold Drive	13	C2
Athold Street	13	C2
Atkinson Court	7	B3
Atkinson Lane	10	B3
Attlee Avenue	35	C2
Attlee Crescent	25	B2
Attlee Grove	5	B2
Attlee Street	7	B3
Audrey Street	13	C3
Audsleys Yard	23	A1
Augusta Court	14	C2
Austin Road	3	A2
Auty Crescent	5	C1
Avens Close	20	A1
Avenue Road	25	B1
Avenue Terrace	19	C1
Avenue, The (Crofton)	26	B1
Avenue, The (Outwood)	5	A2
Avison Yard	15	B2
Avison Yard	T/C	D3
Avon Croft	13	A2
Avon Walk	19	A1
Avondale Drive	5	C1
Avondale Street	15	B2
Avondale Way	15	B2
Aysgarth Close	14	B3
Aysgarth Drive	14	B3

B

Street	Page	Grid
Back Bowman Street	15	C3
Back Church Street	15	C3
Back Duke Of York Street	T/C	E1
Back Duke Street	18	C1
Back Garden Street (Castleford)	2	A2
Back Garden Street (Wakefield)	15	B2
Back Garden Street	T/C	C3
Back Gordon Street	15	C3
Back Grantley Street (Wakefield)	15	B1
Back Grantley Street	T/C	E2
Back Hambleton Street	T/C	D1
Back Hatfeild Street (Wakefield)	15	B1
Back Hatfeild Street	T/C	D1
Back Hatfeild Street (Wakefield)	15	B1
Back Lane (Badsworth)	38	A1
Back Lane (Cold Hiendley)	34	C2
Back Lane (Darrington)	21	A2
Back Lane (Ossett)	13	B2
Back Lane (Sharlston)	17	C3
Back Lane (Upton)	38	B3
Back Lane	15	A1
Back Lane	T/C	B2
Back Lane (Middlestown)	22	B2
Back Mount Pleasant	15	C1
Back Mount Pleasant	T/C	E2
Back Northgate	10	A3
Back Regent Street	15	C3
Back Street	9	C3
Back Walk	10	A2
Back Wesley Street	2	A2
Back Anderton Street	15	C3
Backhouse Lane	32	C3
Bacon Avenue	7	C2
Baden Powell Crescent	20	A1
Badger Close	24	B2
Badsworth Court	38	A1
Badsworth Mews	38	A1
Badsworth View	38	B2
Baghill Court	10	B3
Baghill Lane	10	B3
Bailey Crescent	41	C1
Baileygate Court	10	A3
Baines Mill Yard	23	A1
Baker Lane	5	C1
Balk Avenue	6	A3
Balk Crescent	6	A3
Balk Lane (Netherton)	23	A2
Balk Lane (Wakefield)	6	A3
Balk, The	25	C3
Balmoral Close	19	C2
Balmoral Drive	11	A1
Balne Avenue	15	A1
Balne Avenue	T/C	A2
Balne Lane	15	A1
Balne Lane	T/C	A1
Bamborough Street	16	C3
Bank Street (Castleford)	2	A2
Bank Street (Hemsworth)	37	A3
Bank Street (Horbury)	23	B1
Bank Street (Ossett)	13	B2
Bank Street (Wakefield)	T/C	C2
Bank Wood Road	21	C2
Bank Yard	13	B2
Bankfield Close	13	C2
Bankfield Court	4	C2
Bankfield Drive	4	C2
Banks Avenue (Ackworth)	28	C3
Banks Avenue (Pontefract)	19	C1
Banks Build	19	A2
Banks Garth Cottages	11	C1
Banks Garth	11	C1
Banks Lane	11	C2
Banks Mount	19	C1
Bannockburn Way	6	C2
Baptist Lane	14	A2
Bar Lane (Midgley)	31	A1
Bar Lane (Wakefield)	5	C3
Barden Road	16	A1
Bardwell Court	5	C1
Barewell Hill	36	B3
Barker Road	23	B1
Barker Street	6	B1
Barker's Road	24	B2
Barley Court	23	A3
Barleycorn Close	5	C3
Barleyfield Close	5	C3
Barmby Close	13	C3
Barmby Crescent	13	C3
Barn Court	33	A3
Barnes Avenue	1	C3
Barnes Road	1	C2/2 A3
Barnsdale Close	7	B2
Barnsdale Estate	1	C3
Barnsdale Road	1	A1
Barnsdale Way	39	A3
Barnsley Road (Ackworth)	29	A2
Barnsley Road (Belle Isle)	15	C3
Barnsley Road (Hemsworth)	36	C3
Barnsley Road (Midgley)	31	A2
Barnsley Road (Moorthorpe)	41	A2
Barnsley Road (Newmillerdam)	33	B3

Street	Page	Grid	Street	Page	Grid	Street	Page	Grid	Street	Page	Grid
Barnsley Road (Sandal)	25	A2	Bell Street (North Elmsall)	39	A3	Boundary Lane	17	A1	Broadwell Road	13	C2
Barnstone Vale	5	C3	Bell Street (Wakefield)	15	B1	Bower Hill Lane	31	B2	Brockadale Avenue	20	A2
Barnswick Close	20	A2	Bell Street	T/C	C1	Bowling Avenue	4	C3	Brockswood Court	26	A3
Barratt's Road	5	B3	Belle Isle Avenue	15	C3	Bowman Street	15	C3	Bromley Mount	15	C3
Barstow Square	T/C	C2	Belle Isle Crescent	15	C3	Bowness Avenue	3	A1	Bronte Avenue	3	C3
Barton Way	41	B1	Belle Isle Drive	15	C3	Box Lane	10	B2	Bronte Court	10	A2
Basford Court	15	A2	Belle Vue Road	15	C3	Boycott Drive	29	A3	Bronte Grove	36	C3
Basford Court	T/C	A3	Bellmont Crescent	37	A3	Boycott Way	41	B1	Brook Close	13	C3
Basford Street	15	A2	Belmont Street (Streethouse)	17	C2	Boyne Drive	24	C3	Brook Street (Altofts)	7	A2
Basford Street	T/C	A3	Belmont Street (Wakefield)	5	B3	Boyne Hill (Chapelthorpe)	33	A1	Brook Street (Ossett)	13	B2
Bassenthwaite Walk	11	B2	Belmont Way	41	C2	Boyne Hill (Newmillerdam)	24	C3	Brook Street (Wakefield)	15	B1
Bates Lane	20	B2	Belvoir Drive	11	B1	Bracken Hill (Ackworth)	28	B3	Brook Street	T/C	D2
Batley Road (Alverthorpe)	14	C1	Bembridge Court	14	C2	Bracken Hill (South Kirkby)	41	A2	Brookdale Avenue	13	A1
Batley Road (Kirkhamgate)	4	A3	Benjamin Street	15	A1	Brackenwood Court	5	C1	Brooke Court	20	A2
Baxtergate	10	A3	Benjamin Street	T/C	A1	Brackenwood Road	5	C1	Brookfield Avenue	2	C3
Baylee Street	37	A3	Benjamin Sykes Way	14	A2	Brackhill Bridge	28	B3	Brookfield Court	7	C3
Beacon Drive	38	C2	Bennett Avenue	14	B3	Bradford Road (Newton Bar)	5	A3	Brookfield Drive	29	B2
Beacon Hill	38	B2	Benson Lane	7	C2	Bradford Road (Wrenthorpe)	4	B1	Brookfields	23	C3
Beacon House	38	B3	Bentley Road	14	C2	Bradley Avenue	1	C1	Brooklands Avenue	26	A2
Beacon View	40	C2	Benton Crescent	14	A3	Bradley Carr Terrace	41	B3	Brooklands Court	13	C3
Beaconsfield Road	38	B2	Berne Grove	15	B1	Bradley Street	2	A1	Brooklands Crescent	35	C2
Beal Lane	12	C3	Berne Grove	T/C	D1	Bradwell Lane	13	C2	Brooklands Road	26	A2
Beamshaw	40	C3	Berners Street	15	C1	Braemar Croft	35	C3	Brooklands View	26	A2
Beancroft Road	1	C2	Berners Street	T/C	E2	Braemar Rise	35	C3	Brooksbank	15	A2
Beancroft Street	1	C2	Berry Lane	23	C1	Bramble Close	19	C1	Brooksbank	T/C	B3
Beastfair	10	A3	Berryfield's Garth	13	B1	Bramham Road	1	B2	Brooksfield	41	A2
Beaumont Avenue	41	B2	Berry's Yard	23	B1	Bramley Crescent	5	A2	Brookside Street	41	B2
Beaumont Close	6	A1	Bevan Avenue	7	B3	Bramley Lane	32	A2	Brookside Terrace	41	B2
Beaumont Drive	31	B3	Bevan Place	14	B2	Brampton Court	41	B1	Brookside	37	A3
Beaumont Street	6	A1	Beverley Garth	29	A3	Branch Road	23	C3	Brookway	19	A2
Beck Rise	36	C3	Bevin Close	5	B1	Brand Hill Drive	26	B1	Broom Hall Avenue	5	A3
Beck View	34	A3	Bevin Crescent	5	B1	Brand Hill Approach	26	B1	Broom Hall Crescent	5	A3
Beckbottom Road	4	B2	Bexhill Close	10	B2	Brandy Carr Road	4	B2	Broomcroft Road	13	B3
Beckbridge Court	7	C2	Billingham Close	4	B3	Bransdale Avenue	7	B2	Broome Close	7	B2
Beckbridge Green	7	C2	Binks Street	5	B2	Bransdale Mews	7	A2	Broomhill Avenue	12	A2
Beckbridge Lane	7	C3	Binks Yard	13	B2	Branstone Grove	13	B1	Broomhill Close	12	A2
Beckbridge Road	7	C2	Birch Green	10	B3	Brazil Street	2	A1	Broomhill Crescent	12	A2
Beckbridge Way	7	C3	Birch Grove	3	A2	Bread Street	T/C	D2	Broomhill Drive	12	A2
Beckett Close	14	B3	Birch Road	17	B1	Bredon Close	37	B3	Broomhill Grove	12	A2
Beckley Road	15	A1	Birch Street	15	C2	Brentlea Avenue	15	B3	Broomhill Place	12	A2
Bective Road	14	B1	Birch Tree Walk	11	B2	Brentwood Close	30	B3	Broomhill Square	12	A2
Bedale Drive	11	B2	Birchen Avenue	13	A2	Brettegate	36	C3	Broomhill Walk	12	A2
Bede Court	5	B3	Birchen Hills	13	A2	Bretton Lane (West Bretton)	31	C2	Broomhill	2	B2
Bedford Close (Crofton)	26	C1	Birchtree Close	5	C3	Bretton Lane	32	A1	Brotherton Avenue	15	C1
Bedford Close (Purston Jaglin)	19	A3	Bird Lane	40	C3	Brevitt Street	15	C3	Brotherton Avenue	T/C	F1
Bedford Court	19	A2	Birkhill	2	C2	Brewery Lane	11	C1	Brownhill Crescent	36	B1
Beech Avenue (New Crofton)	27	A2	Birkdale Road	34	B3	Briar Bank	36	B1	Brunel Road	4	C2
Beech Avenue (Stanley)	5	C2	Birkwood Avenue	17	B3	Briar Grove	15	C3	Brunswick Grove	T/C	E2
Beech Avenue (Wakefield)	14	C1	Birkwood Road	6	B2	Briarwood Close	5	B2	Brunswick Street	15	C2
Beech Close	40	B3	Black Road	16	B3	Brick Street	14	B1	Brunswick Street	T/C	E2
Beech Court (Castleford)	2	A2	Blackburn Court	19	C1	Bridge Close	23	A1	Brunswick	35	B1
Beech Court (Ossett)	13	A2	Blackburn Lane	12	A2	Bridge Court	36	B1	Bryan Close	1	B2
Beech Crescent (Castleford)	3	A3	Blacker Crescent	23	A2	Bridge Lane (Knottingley)	11	C1	Buckingham Court	16	A3
Beech Crescent (Darrington)	21	A2	Blacker Lane (Crigglestone)	19	C3	Bridge Lane (Thorpe Audlin)	30	B3	Buckingham Drive	16	A3
Beech Croft	25	C2	Blacker Lane (Netherton)	23	A2	Bridge Road	23	A1	Buckingham Way	16	A3
Beech Drive	29	A1	Blackthorn Way	15	A1	Bridge Street (Castleford)	2	A1	Buckle Lane	7	A3
Beech Gardens	3	A3	Blakeley Grove	14	C1	Bridge Street (Normanton)	7	C2	Bugler Terrace	23	A1
Beech Grove (Featherstone)	19	A2	Blakey Road	14	C1	Bridge Street (Pontefract)	10	A3	Builds Lane	12	A1
Beech Grove (Kinsley)	36	B1	Bland's Close	2	A2	Bridge Street (Wakefield)	15	C2	Bull Lane (Crigglestone)	24	B3
Beech Grove (Normanton)	7	B3	Bleakley Avenue	34	B3	Bridle Avenue	13	A1	Bull Lane (South Kirkby)	40	C2
Beech Hill	10	B3	Bleakley Terrace	34	B3	Bridle Close	23	A2	Bullenshaw Road	37	A3
Beech Road	38	B3	Bleasdale Avenue	11	B1	Bridle Lane (Gawthorpe)	13	A1	Bullenshaw Villas	37	C3
Beech Street (Pontefract)	20	A1	Blenheim Close	11	A1	Bridle Lane (Netherton)	23	A2	Bullring	15	B1
Beech Street (South Elmsall)	41	A3	Blenheim Road	5	B3	Bridle Place	13	B1	Bullring	T/C	C2
Beech Tree Road	19	A2	Blind Lane	34	C2	Brier Lane	35	B2	Bullstyle Road	19	C2
Beech View	32	C1	Blue Butts	13	A2	Brierley Crescent	40	C2	Bunkers Hill	4	C3
Beechfield	25	B1	Bluebell Close	20	A1	Brierley Road	36	A3	Burkill Street	15	C3
Beechlands	20	B2	Blundell Street	41	A2	Brigg's Avenue	2	A2	Burnhill Lane	30	A3
Beechnut Lane	9	C3	Blyton Way	3	A3	Briggs Row	19	A2	Burns Avenue	40	B3
Beechwood Avenue (Flanshaw)	14	B2	Bodmin Drive	7	B2	Brighton Street	15	A2	Burntwood Lane	40	A3
Beechwood Avenue (Pontefract)	19	C1	Bolton Wife Hill	32	C2	Brighton Street	T/C	A3	Burntwood Avenue	40	C3
Beechwood Crescent (Hemsworth)	36	C3	Bolus Close	5	B2	Brindle Park Drive	2	B2	Burntwood Bank	36	C3
			Bolus Lane	5	B2	Brindley Way	4	C2	Burntwood Crescent	40	C3
Beechwood Crescent (Pontefract)	19	C1	Bond Street (Pontefract)	10	B2	Broad Cut Road	24	A2	Burntwood Drive	40	C3
Beechwood Dale	29	B2	Bond Street (Wakefield)	15	B1	Broad Lane	40	B3	Burrell Street	15	C1
Beechwood Grove	23	C1	Bond Street	T/C	C1	Broad View	13	C2	Burrell Street	T/C	E2
Beechwood Mount	36	C3	Bond Terrace	T/C	C1	Broad Acres	24	B2	Burton Street (South Elmsall)	41	B2
Beechwood	19	C1	Bondgate	10	B3	Broadacre Road	13	C2	Burton Street (Wakefield)	15	B1
Belfry Court	5	B2	Booth Street	1	C2	Broadgate	13	C2	Burton Street	T/C	C2
Belgrave Avenue	13	B2	Booths	10	B3	Broadheads Yard	13	B2	Bush Street	37	C3
Belgrave Mount	5	B3	Borough Road	15	B1	Broadmead	2	B1	Butcher Hill	37	A2
Belgrave Street	13	B2	Borough Road	T/C	D1	Broadmeadows	5	B1	Butcher's Gap Lane	17	B1
Belgrave Terrace	5	B3	Borrowdale Drive	3	A1	Broadowler Lane	13	C2	Buttermere Croft	25	C2
Belgravia Road	15	A1	Borrowdale Road	14	C1	Broadway (Lupset)	14	B2	Buttermere Walk	11	B3
Belks Court	10	A3	Boston Street	2	A1	Broadway (Pontefract)	20	B1	Button Park	20	A1
Bell Lane	28	C3	Bosworth Avenue	6	C2	Broadway (South Elmsall)	41	A3	Butts Lane	22	B2
			Bottom Boat Road	6	B1	Broadway Terrace	41	A3	Butts, The	10	A3

Street	Map	Grid
Buxton Place	5	A3
Byron Close	3	C3
Byron Grove	5	C1
Byways, The	20	A1

C

Street	Map	Grid
Calder Close (Ossett)	13	A2
Calder Close (Castleford)	2	C1
Calder Mount	24	A3
Calder Street (Castleford)	1	C1
Calder Street (Wakefield)	15	B2
Calder Terrace	23	C1
Calder Vale Road	15	C2
Calder Vale Road	T/C	F3
Calder View (Ossett)	13	A2
Calder View (Crigglestone)	24	A3
Caledonia Court	4	A3
California Drive (Horbury)	23	C1
California Drive (Normanton)	7	C1
Calverley Green Road	7	A2
Calverts Walk	13	C2
Cambridge Crescent	16	B3
Cambridge Street (Castleford)	2	A2
Cambridge Street (Normanton)	7	B3
Cambridge Street (South Elmsall)	41	A2
Cambridge Street (Wakefield)	15	B2
Camden Road	3	A2
Camellia Close	14	B3
Camelot Close	10	A3
Camp Mount	9	C3
Camp Rise	9	C3
Camp Road	40	B3
Campion Close	20	A1
Canal Court	5	B1
Canal Lane	5	C1
Canning Avenue	4	B3
Cannon Street	2	A3
Cardigan Lane	13	C3
Cardigan Terrace	T/C	C1
Cardwell Terrace	12	A1
Carleton Close	20	A1
Carleton Crest	20	A1
Carleton Gate	20	A1
Carleton Glen	20	A1
Carleton Green Close	20	B2
Carleton Green Stables	20	B2
Carleton Park Avenue	20	A1
Carleton Park Road	20	A1
Carleton Road (Darrington)	20	C2
Carleton Road (Pontefract)	20	A1/B2
Carleton View	20	A1
Carlton Avenue	2	B2
Carlton Close (Normanton)	7	B3
Carlton Close (Hemsworth)	36	C3
Carlton Court (Ossett)	13	B2
Carlton Court (South Elmsall)	41	B2
Carlton Croft	25	A2
Carlton Gardens	41	B2
Carlton Road	41	B2
Carlton Street (Castleford)	2	A1
Carlton Street (Featherstone)	19	A1
Carlton Street (Horbury)	23	B1
Carlton Street (Normanton)	7	B2
Carlton Street (Wakefield)	15	A2
Carlton Street	T/C	A3
Carlyle Crescent	2	C2
Carlyle Road	2	C2
Carnlea Grove	15	B3
Carr Gate Crescent	4	B1
Carr Gate Drive	4	B1
Carr Gate Mount	4	B1
Carr Lane (Castleford)	2	B3
Carr Lane (Fitzwilliam)	36	A1
Carr Lane (Middlestown)	22	B3
Carr Lane (Sandal)	25	A2
Carr Lane (South Kirkby)	40	C2
Carr Lane Avenue	2	B3
Carr View	40	C2
Carr Wood Road	2	B3
Carrgate	36	B1
Carroll Court	41	B2
Carter Street	15	B1
Carter Street	T/C	C2
Castle Avenue	25	A1
Castle Chain	10	A3
Castle Crescent	25	A2
Castle Garth	10	B3
Castle Grove	23	C1
Castle Hill	14	B2
Castle Parade	2	B3
Castle Road West	25	A1
Castle Road	25	B1
Castle Street	14	C2
Castle Syke Hill	19	C2
Castle Terrace	25	A1
Castle Vale	10	B2
Castle View (Horbury)	23	C1
Castle View (Sandal)	25	A2
Castle View (Pontefract)	10	A3
Castlefield Court	2	A2
Castleford Lane (Ackton)	8	B2
Castleford Lane (Ferrybridge)	11	A1
Castleford Road	7	C2
Castlegate Drive	19	C1
Castlesyke View	20	A2
Cathedral Close	T/C	B1
Catherine Street	28	A3
Catlow Street	1	C2
Cattlelaith Lane	11	A2
Causeway Garth Lane	30	B3
Cave Crescent	14	C2
Cavewell Close	13	C3
Cavewell Gardens	13	C3
Cawthorne Road	24	C3
Cedar Avenue	13	B3
Cedar Close	19	C2
Cedar Court	2	A2
Cedar Drive	13	A2
Cedar Grove	19	A1
Cedar Road	17	B1
Cedar Walk (Knottingley)	11	B2
Cedar Walk (Featherstone)	19	A1
Celandine Close	20	A1
Cemetery Road (Hemsworth)	36	C2
Cemetery Road (Normanton)	7	C2
Cemetery Road (Ryhill)	35	B2
Central Avenue (Fitzwilliam)	28	A3
Central Avenue (South Elmsall)	41	B3
Central Drive	1	B2
Centre Street (Hemsworth)	37	A2
Centre Street (South Elmsall)	41	B2
Chain Street	1	C2
Chald Lane	15	A2
Chald Lane	T/C	B3
Chancery Lane (Osset)	13	A1
Chancery Lane (Wakefield)	T/C	C2
Chancery Road	13	A1
Chandlers Close	5	A1
Chantry Close	19	C1
Chantry Croft	36	B1
Chantry Road	14	C2
Chantry Street	14	C2
Chapel Close	27	C2
Chapel Fold	5	A2
Chapel Garth	29	A3
Chapel Hill Lane	22	B3
Chapel Lane (Badsworth)	38	A1
Chapel Lane (South Elmsall)	41	C2
Chapel Street (Knottingley)	11	C1
Chapel Street (Ossett Spa)	13	C3
Chapel Street (Ryhill)	35	B2
Chapel Street (Stanley)	5	C1
Chapelfields	40	B3
Chariot Way	30	B3
Charles Avenue (Agbrigg)	16	A3
Charles Avenue (Outwood)	5	B1
Charles Cotton Close	4	B3
Charles Street (Castleford)	2	A2
Charles Street (Horbury)	24	A2
Charles Street (Ossett)	13	C3
Charles Street (Ryhill)	35	B2
Charles Street (South Hiendley)	36	A3
Charles Street (Wakefield)	15	C2
Charles Street	T/C	E3
Charlestown Estate	29	A3
Charlesworth Court	15	A2
Charlesworth Court	T/C	C3
Charlesworth Way	15	A2
Charlesworth Way	T/C	B3
Charlesworth Place	6	B1
Charlesworths Buildings	23	B1
Charleville	41	A2
Charlotte Grove	13	C3
Charlotte Street	15	B2
Charlotte Street	T/C	D3
Chase, The	6	A1
Chaucer Avenue	5	C1
Cheapside (Normanton)	7	B3
Cheapside (Wakefield)	15	B1
Cheapside	T/C	C2
Chequerfield Avenue	20	B1
Chequerfield Close	1	B3
Chequerfield Drive	20	B1
Chequerfield Lane	10	B3
Chequerfield Mount	20	B1
Chequerfield Road	20	B1
Chequers Close	20	B1
Chequers Court	20	B1
Cherry Garth	36	C3
Cherry Tree Avenue	11	B2
Cherry Tree Crescent	26	A2
Cherry Tree Drive	26	A2
Cherry Tree Road	26	A2
Chesterton Court	14	B3
Chestnut Avenue	25	C2
Chestnut Close	23	C1
Chestnut Crescent	17	B1
Chestnut Drive	35	C3
Chestnut Green	10	B3
Chestnut Grove (Pontefract)	20	A1
Chestnut Grove (Crofton)	26	B1
Chestnut Grove (Hemsworth)	37	B3
Chestnut Street	41	B3
Chestnut Walk (Knottingley)	11	B2
Chestnut Walk (Wakefield)	15	A1
Chestnuts, The	3	C3/C2
Chevet Court	25	A2
Chevet Croft	25	B2
Chevet Grange	34	A1
Chevet Grove	25	B2
Chevet Hill	34	A1
Chevet Lane (Notton)	34	B2
Chevet Lane (Sandal)	25	B2/B3
Chevet Park	33	C1
Chevet Terrace	25	C1
Cheviot Close	37	A3
Cheviot Drive	37	B3
Cheviot Place	11	B1
Childs Road	4	B3
Childswell Lane	13	A1
Chiltern Avenue (Ferrybridge)	11	B1
Chiltern Avenue (Whitwood)	1	A3
Chiltern Court (Ackworth)	29	A3
Chiltern Court (Hemsworth)	37	B3
Chiltern Drive	29	A3
Church Avenue (Kirkthorpe)	16	C1
Church Avenue (South Kirkby)	40	C2
Church Close (Hemsworth)	37	A2
Church Close (Sharlston)	17	B3
Church Court	7	B3
Church Crescent	23	A2
Church Drive	40	C2
Church Farm Close	7	A2
Church Fields (Normanton)	7	B3
Church Fields (Ryhill)	35	B1
Church Garth	2	B2
Church Grove	40	C2
Church Lane (Chapelthorpe)	24	B3
Church Lane (Cold Hiendley)	35	A2
Church Lane (Darrington)	21	A2
Church Lane (East Hardwick)	29	C1
Church Lane (Featherstone)	8	C3
Church Lane (Horbury)	23	C1
Church Lane (Netherton)	23	A2
Church Lane (Normanton)	7	B3
Church Lane (Outwood)	5	A1
Church Lane (Pontefract)	10	A3
Church Lane (Snydale)	7	C3
Church Lane Avenue	5	A2
Church Mount	40	C3
Church Road (Altofts)	7	A2
Church Road (Stanley)	6	A1
Church Street (Castleford)	1	C1
Church Street (Horbury)	23	B1
Church Street (Ossett)	13	B1
Church Street (South Elmsall)	41	C2
Church Street (Wakefield)	15	B2
Church Street (Woolley)	32	C3
Church Top	40	C3
Church View (Castleford)	1	C2
Church View (Crigglestone)	24	B3
Church View (Sandal)	15	C3
Church View (South Kirkby)	40	C2
Church View Close	35	C2
Church Villas	40	C3
Church Way	26	C1
Churchbalk Drive	20	B1
Churchbalk Lane	20	B1
Churchfield Croft	7	A2
Churchfield Lane	2	B2
Churchfields (Crofton)	26	C1
Churchfields (Ryhill)	35	B2
Churchill Grove	25	B2
Churwell Close	2	A2
Cinder Lane	1	C1
Circle, The	20	B1
Claremont Street	15	C3
Claremont Terrace	15	A2
Claremont Terrace	T/C	A3
Claremount Crescent	26	C1
Clarence Road	15	B3
Clarendon Cottages	13	B3
Clarendon Court	15	B1
Clarendon Court	T/C	D1
Clarendon Street	15	B1
Clarion Street	15	C2
Clark Crescent	17	A1
Clarke Grove	5	C3
Clarkson Street	15	A2
Clarkson Street	T/C	B3
Clarkson Court	7	C3
Clarkson Street	15	A2
Clayfield Bungalows	11	A1
Clayton Avenue	39	A2
Clayton Cottages	23	B1
Clayton Court	18	C2
Clayton Holt	40	C3
Clayton Mews	7	A2
Clayton Place	7	A2
Clayton Rise	5	A1
Clayton View	40	B3
Claytons Buildings	9	A3
Cleevethorpe Grove	25	B1
Clement Street	14	C2
Cleveland Avenue (Knottingley)	11	B2
Cleveland Avenue (Lupset)	14	B3
Cleveland Garth	14	B3
Cleveland Grove	14	B3
Cliff Drive	24	A3
Cliff Grove	23	C3
Cliff Hill	15	A1
Cliff Hill	T/C	B1
Cliff Lane	15	A1
Cliff Lane	T/C	C2
Cliff Parade	15	B1
Cliff Parade	T/C	C2
Cliff Park Avenue	15	A1
Cliff Park Avenue	T/C	B1
Cliff Road	23 C3/24 A3	
Cliff Side	12	A2
Cliff Street (Pontefract)	19	C1
Cliff Street (Wakefield)	14	C1
Cliffe Crest	14	A3
Clifford Avenue	15	B3
Clifford Court	13	A2
Clifford Road	40	B2
Clifford Street	41	B2
Clifford View	15	B3
Clifton Avenue (Horbury)	13	C3
Clifton Avenue (Pontefract)	9	C3
Clifton Avenue (Stanley)	5	C2
Clifton Close	23	B1
Clifton Drive	13	C3
Clifton Place	5	A3
Clifton Road (Horbury)	23	B1
Clifton Road (Sharlston)	17	B3
Clifton Street	36	C3
Clifton View	9	C3
Clock Row Avenue	41	A2
Clock Row Grove	41	A2
Clock Row Mount	41	A2
Close Road	2	B2
Close Street	36	C2
Close, The (Durkar)	24	B2
Close, The (Pontefract)	20	B1
Club Terrace	36	B1

Street	Page	Grid
Clubhouses Croft	23	B1
Cluntergate	23	C1
Clyde Street	15	C3
Co-Operative Street (Horbury)	23	B1
Co-Operative Street (Wakefield)	15	A2
Co-Operative Street	T/C	A3
Coach Road	5	B2
Coal Pit Lane	39	B1
Cobb Avenue	14	C2
Cobbler Hall	31	C2
Cobbler's Lane	10	B2
Cobham Parade	5	B2
Cock Lane (Sharlston)	17	A3
Cock Lane (Crofton)	26	B1
Cockpit Lane	10	A3
Colbeck Street	14	B1
Cold Hiendley Common Lane	34	C2
Coleridge Crescent	4	C2
Coleridge Way	10	A2
Colin Barnaby Court	14	B1
Colinsway	15	A2
Colleen Road	24	A3
College Grove (Castleford)	1	B2
College Grove (Wakefield)	15	B1
College Grove Close (Wakefield)	15	B1
College Grove Road	15	B1
College Grove Road	T/C	C1
College Grove View	15	B1
College Road	2	C2
College Terrace	28	C3
College View	28	C2
Colliery Approach	5	A1
Collingwood Road	7	B2
Colonel's Walk	10	A3
Coltsfoot Close	20	A1
Colwyn Terrace	19	A1
Commercial Street (Castleford)	2	A1
Commercial Street (Wakefield)	15	B2
Common Ing Lane	35	B1
Common Lane (Knottingley)	12	A2
Common Lane (Thorpe Audlin)	38	C1
Common Lane (Upton)	38	B3
Common Lane (Walton)	25	B3
Common Lane (Woolley)	32	B2
Common Road (Kinsley)	36	B1
Common Road (Lofthouse Gate)	5	C1
Common Road (South Kirkby)	40	B3
Common Road Avenue	40	B3
Common Side Lane	18	B1
Coniston Court	5	B1
Coniston Drive	3	A2
Coniston Gardens	3	A2
Coniston Place	11	B3
Conistone Crescent	5	C3
Constable Grove	5	C1
Convent Avenue	40	C2
Conway Road	14	C1
Conyers Yard	13	B2
Cooksland Lane	18	A1
Cookson Close	3	A3
Copeworth Drive	32	C1
Copper Beech Close	20	A1
Copper Beech Court	25	C2
Coppice Close	5	C3
Copse, The	8	C3
Corn Market	10	A3
Coronation Avenue	7	A2
Coronation Bungalows	11	B1
Coronation Estate	38	B3
Coronation Road	17	B3
Coronation Street (Castleford)	2	B1
Coronation Street (Glass Houghton)	2	B2
Coronation Street (Wrenthorpe)	4	C3
Coronation Terrace	2	B2
Cosy Nook	40	C2
Cotswold Close	37	B3
Cotswold Drive	11	B1
Cotswold Road	14	B2
Cottam Croft	37	A3
Cotterill Road	11	A2
Cotton Street	15	B2
Coupe Grove	7	A2
Court Way, The	29	B2
Courtyard, The	33	A3
Cow Lane (Havercroft)	35	B2
Cow Lane (Knottingley)	11	C1
Cow Lane (Sharlston)	17	B2
Coxley Crescent	22	C3
Coxley Lane	22	C2
Coxley View	22	C3
Crab Hill	10	A3
Crab Lane	24	C3
Crab Tree Lane	39	C1
Crag Mount	9	C3
Craven Road	36	C3
Craven Street	15	B1
Craven Street	T/C	D1
Crawford Drive	14	C1
Crawley Avenue	41	A2
Crayford Drive	26	C1
Crescent Road	35	C2
Crescent, The (Altofts)	7	A2
Crescent, The (Castleford)	2	B2
Crescent, The (Netherton)	22	C3
Crescent, The (Streethouse)	17	C2
Crest Drive	20	B1
Crest Mount	20	B1
Crewe Road	3	A2
Cricketers Close	29	A3
Cricketers Approach	4	C2
Crinan Court	7	B2
Croft Avenue (Altofts)	7	A2
Croft Avenue (Knottingley)	11	C1
Croft Avenue (Normanton)	7	C2
Croft Head Lane	17	A1
Croft, The (Badsworth)	38	A1
Croft, The (Castleford)	2	B2
Croft, The (Knottingley)	11	C1
Croft, The (West Bretton)	31	C2
Croftlands	11	C1
Cromwell Crescent	10	B3
Cromwell Place	13	B2
Cromwell Road	3	A2
Cross Hands Lane	28	A2
Cross Hill Lane	36	A2
Cross Hill	37	A2
Cross Keys	13	C1
Cross Keys Court	23	B1
Cross Lane	14	C2
Cross Normanton Street	23	C1
Cross Park Avenue	2	B2
Cross Park Street	23	B1
Cross Pipes Road	14	C1
Cross Queen Street	7	B3
Cross Road (Chapelthorpe)	32	C1
Cross Road (Middlestown)	22	B2
Cross Ryecroft Street	13	A2
Cross Square	T/C	C2/D2
Cross Street (Castleford)	1	C1
Cross Street (Gawthorpe)	13	A1
Cross Street (Hemsworth)	36	C3
Cross Street (Horbury)	23	C1
Cross Street (North Elmsall)	39	A2
Cross Street (Pontefract)	10	A3
Cross Street (Wakefield)	15	B1
Cross Street	T/C	C2
Crossfield Court	22	A2
Crossfields	22	A2
Crossley Street (Featherstone)	19	A2
Crossley Street (New Sharlston)	17	A2
Crossman Drive	7	C2
Crowcrowns Lane	10	C2
Crown Court	T/C	C2
Crown Point Close	13	A2
Crown Point Drive	13	A2
Crown Point Road	13	A2
Crown Street	13	B3
Crown And Anchor Yard	10	A3
Crownlands Lane	13	B2
Crowther Place	1	C2
Crowther Street	1	C2
Croxall Drive	5	C1
Crummock Place	11	B2
Crystal Place	T/C	E3
Cubley Avenue	24	C3
Cumberland Road	3	A1
Cumbrian Way	14	C3
Curlew Close	2	A3
Cutsyke Avenue	1	C3
Cutsyke Crest	1	C3
Cutsyke Hill	1	C2
Cutsyke Road	8	C2
Cutsyke Walk	1	C3
Cypress Road	7	B3
Cyprus Avenue	5	A3
Cyprus Grove	5	A3
Cyprus Mount	5	A3
Cyprus Street (Gawthorpe)	13	A1
Cyprus Street (Wakefield)	5	A3

D

Street	Page	Grid
Dacre Avenue	14	B2
Dahl Drive	3	A3
Dale Close	13	B2
Dale Court	20	A2
Dale Lane	41	C1
Dale Mews	20	A2
Dale Street	13	B2
Dale View (Hemsworth)	37	B3
Dale View (Pontefract)	20	A2
Dale Walk	18	C3
Dalefield Avenue	7	B3
Dalefield Road	7	B3
Dalton Terrace	1	C2
Danby Lane	25	A3
Dandy Mill Avenue	10	B2
Dandy Mill Croft	10	B2
Dandy Mill View	10	B2
Danella Crescent	4	C2
Danella Grove	4	C2
Danes Lane	22	B2
Danesleigh Drive	22	B2
Dark Lane	20	A1
Darkfield Lane	3	B3
Darning Lane	30	B3
Darnley Avenue	15	A1
Darnley Avenue	T/C	A1
Darrington Lane	29	C1
Darrington Road	20	B3
David Street (Castleford)	1	C2
David Street (Wakefield)	15	C3
Davis Avenue	3	A2
Daw Green Avenue	24	A3
Daw Lane	23	C1
Dawes Avenue	2	B2
Dawtrie Close	3	A2
Dawtrie Street	3	A2
De Lacy Avenue	8	C3
De Lacy Crescent	3	A1
De Lacy Terrace	10	B3
Dean Close	4	C3
Dearden Street	13	B2
Dearne Street	41	B2
Deffer Road	24	C3
Delph, The	19	B2
Denby Crest	21	A2
Denby Dale Road (Bretton)	31	C1/32 A1
Denby Dale Road (Calder Grove)	23	C3
Denby Dale Road (Durkar)	24	B2
Denby Dale Road (Wakefield)	15	B2
Denby Dale Road	T/C	C3
Denby Dale Road East	24	B2
Denby Dale Road West	24	A2
Denby Road	21	A2
Deneside	13	A1
Denhale Avenue	14	C2
Denholme Drive	13	B1
Denholme Meadow	41	B1
Denmark Street	15	C3
Dennington Lane	32	B1
Denstone Street	15	B1
Denstone Street	T/C	E1
Dent Drive	6	A3
Denton Gardens	29	A3
Denton Terrace	2	A1
Denwell Terrace	10	A3
Derwent Drive	3	B1
Derwent Grove	14	C1
Derwent Place	11	B3
Derwent Road	14	C1
Devon Grove	13	A2
Devonshire Court (Gawthorpe)	11	C1
Dewsbury Road (Ossett)	13	A1
Dewsbury Road	14	B2
Diamond Avenue	41	A2
Dicky Sykes Lane	28	B3
Dickinson Court	15	B3
Dickinson Street	15	B1
Dickinson Street	T/C	D1
Dickinson Terrace	19	A1
Dimple Gardens	13	B3
Dimple Wells Close	13	B2
Dimple Wells Road	13	B2
Dixon Street (Castleford)	1	C2
Dixon Street (Featherstone)	19	A1
Dixon's Yard	15	B2
Dodsworth Crescent	17	B1
Dodworth Drive	24	C3
Don Pedro Avenue	7	C3
Don Pedro Close	7	C3
Doncaster Road (Ackworth)	29	A3
Doncaster Road (Badsworth)	37	C1
Doncaster Road (Crofton)	26	C1
Doncaster Road (Foulby)	27	B1
Doncaster Road (Knottingley)	11	A1
Doncaster Road (Sharlston)	16	B3
Doncaster Road (South Elmsall)	41	C3
Doncaster Road (Upton)	38	B3
Doncaster Road (Wakefield)	15	C2
Doncaster Road Estate	29	A3
Dorchester Avenue	9	C3
Dorman Avenue	39	A3
Dorset Close	37	A2
Dovecote Close	14	A3
Dovecote Garden	10	A3
Dovecote Lane	23	B1
Dovedale Close	26	C1
Downland Crescent	12	A2
Drivers Row	19	C1
Drove Drive	2	C1
Drury Lane (Altofts)	7	A2
Drury Lane (Wakefield)	15	B1
Drury Lane	T/C	C2
Dudfleet Lane	23	C1
Duke Of York Avenue (Sandal)	25	A1
Duke Of York Avenue (Wakefield)	15	B3
Duke Of York Street (Wakefield)	15	B1
Duke Of York Street	T/C	E1
Duke Of York Street (Wrenthorpe)	4	C3
Duke Street (Fitzwilliam)	36	B1
Duke Street (Castleford)	2	A1
Duke Street (Whitwood Mere)	1	C1
Dulverton Close	10	B2
Dulverton Rise	10	B2
Dulverton Way	10	B2
Dunbar Street	15	C3
Duncan Avenue	25	B1
Dunderdale Crescent	3	A1
Dunlands Lane	22	B2
Dunn Close	4	C2
Dunsil Villas	41	B3
Dunsley Lane	40	A2
Dunsley Terrace	40	B3
Dunstan Close	13	C3
Durham Street	2	A3
Durkar Court	24	B2
Durkar Fields	24	B2
Durkar Lane	24	B2
Durkar Low Lane	24	B2
Durkar Rise	24	B3

E

Street	Page	Grid
Eagle Grove	14	B1
Earl Street (Fitzwilliam)	36	B1
Earl Street (Wakefield)	15	B1
Earl Street	T/C	E1
Earle Street	18	C1
Earnshaw Place	15	A1
Earnshaw Place	T/C	C1
East Avenue (Horbury)	23	C1
East Avenue (Pontefract)	19	C1
East Avenue (South Elmsall)	41	C1
East Avenue (Upton)	38	B3
East Close	20	B2
East Dale Close	37	B2
East Down	2	B1

Street	Map	Grid
East Drive	20	B1
East Street (Havercroft)	35	C2
East Street (Newton Hill)	5	B3
East Street (South Elmsall)	41	C1
East Street (South Hiendley)	36	A3
East Street (Stanley)	6	A3
East View (Knottingley)	11	C1
East View (Ossett)	13	C3
East View (Whitwood Mere)	1	B2
Eastbourne Avenue	19	A1
Eastbourne Close	20	C1
Eastbourne Crescent	20	C1
Eastbourne Drive	20	C1
Eastbourne Terrace	10	B3
Eastbourne View	10	B3
Eastfield Avenue	11	C2
Eastfield Drive	10	B3
Eastfield Grove	7	C2
Eastfield Lane	2	A1
Eastfield Road	11	C2
Eastgate	37	A3
Eastmoor Road	5 B3/15	B1
Eastmount	35	B2
Eastville Road	17	B3
Eastwood Avenue	14	C1
Eastwood Close	24	B2
Eaton Place	37	A2
Eaton Walk	41	B1
Eddystone Rise	11	B2
Edelshain Grove	25	B2
Eden Avenue (Lupset)	14	B2
Eden Avenue (Ossett)	13	B2
Edendale	2	B1
Edgemoor Road	32	C1
Edna Street	41	B2
Edward Court	4	C2
Edward Drive	5	B1
Edward Street (Altofts)	7	B1
Edward Street (Wakefield)	T/C	E1
Elba Terrace	14	A3
Elder Avenue (Upton)	38	C2
Elder Avenue (Wakefield)	15	A1
Elder Drive	38	C2
Elder Green	15	A1
Elder Green	T/C	A1
Elder Grove	15	A1
Elder Grove	T/C	A2
Elder Street	T/C	A1
Eldon Street	13	C1
Eliots Close	3	A3
Elizabeth Avenue	36	A3
Elizabeth Court	37	B3
Elizabeth Drive (Castleford)	3	A1
Elizabeth Drive (Knottingley)	11	A1
Elizabeth Gardens	5	B3
Elizabeth Street	15	C3
Elizabethan Court	10	B2
Ella Street	28	A3
Elland Street	2	A1
Ellentrees Lane	7	B2
Ellin's Terrace	7	A3
Ellis Laithe Fold	35	A3
Ellis Street	23	B1
Elm Avenue	6	A2
Elm Close (Darrington)	21	A2
Elm Close (South Ossett)	13	B3
Elm Gardens	3	A3
Elm Grove	41	B2
Elm Mews	23	C1
Elm Park	20	A1
Elm Place	11	B2
Elm Road (Hemsworth)	37	A3
Elm Road (Woodhouse)	17	B1
Elm Street	27	A2
Elm Terrace	10	A3
Elm Tree Street	15	C3
Elms, The	29	A3
Elmete Road	3	A1
Elmhurst Grove	11	B2
Elmsall Lane	41	C3
Elmsdale Close	41	C3
Elmwood Avenue	26	A2
Elmwood Close	25	C2
Elmwood Drive	25	C2
Elmwood Garth	26	A2
Elmwood Grove	23	C1
Elsicker Lane	17	A1
Elstone View	5	A2
Elvey Street	15	B1
Emblem Terrace	15	C3
Emily Street	41	A2
Engine Lane (Horbury)	23	A1
Engine Lane (Wragby)	27	C2
England Lane	11	C2
Ennerdale Drive	11	B3
Ennerdale Road	14	C1
Enterprise Way	1	C2
Eric Street	41	B2
Esk Avenue	2	C1
Eskdale Avenue	7	B2
Eskdale Close	7	B2
Eskdale Court	7	B2
Eskdale Croft	7	B2
Eskdale Road	14	C1
Estcourt Drive	21	B2
Estcourt Road	21	A2
Esther Avenue	14	C2
Esther Grove	14	C2
Everdale Mount (Hemsworth)	36	C3
Everdale Mount (South Elmsall)	41	A2
Exchange Street (Normanton)	7	B3
Exchange Street (South Elmsall)	41	B2
Express Way	7	C1

F

Street	Map	Grid
Fair Fields	3	A2
Fair View (Pontefract)	20	B2
Fair View (Ackworth)	29	A3
Fairbrook Road	24	B3
Fairburn Street	1	C1
Fairfax Avenue (Featherstone)	8	C3
Fairfax Avenue (Knottingley)	11	B2
Fairfax Road	10	B3
Fairfield Avenue (Altofts)	6	C2
Fairfield Avenue (Ossett)	13	C3
Fairfield Avenue (Pontefract)	19	C1
Fairfield Close (Castleford)	3	A1
Fairfield Close (Ossett)	13	C2
Fairfield Court	2	B2
Fairfield Drive	13	C2
Fairfield Gardens	13	C2
Fairfield Mount	13	C3
Fairfield Road	13	C2
Fairfield Terrace	13	C3
Fairfield Walk	13	C2
Fairway Avenue	7	C3
Fairway Close	7	C3
Fairway Drive	7	C3
Fairway Gardens	7	C3
Fairway Meadows	7	C3
Fairway, The	9	A3
Fairway Approach	7	C3
Fairway	7	C3
Fairways Court	21	B2
Fairy Hill Lane	3	A3
Faith Street	41	A2
Falcon Drive	1	C2
Fall Ings Road	15	C2
Falmouth Avenue	7	B2
Falmouth Crescent	7	B2
Far Richard Close	13	B1
Farfield Court	41	B1
Farfield Lane	35	C2
Farm Croft	18	A2
Farm Gardens	18	A2
Farm Lane	36	B1
Farm Road	19	A2
Farmfield Drive	36	B1
Farne Avenue	14	C2
Farnham Way	26	C1
Farriers Place	2	C2
Favell Avenue	7	B3
Fawcett Street	15	B3
Fearnley Avenue	13	A1
Fearnley Drive	13	A1
Fearnley Street	18	C2
Fearnsides Close	23	B1
Featherstone Lane (Featherstone)	9	A3
Featherstone Lane (Pontefract)	19	A1
Fellowsides Lane	13	B2
Fellowsides Mews	13	B2
Fenton Close	40	C3
Fenton Road	5	C1
Fern Croft	4	C2
Fernandes Place	23	A1
Ferndale Place	36	C3
Ferndale	19	A2
Fernlea Close	26	C1
Fernleigh Court	14	C2
Fernley Green Close	12	A1
Fernley Green Road	12	A1
Fernley Hill Drive	7	A1
Fernley Villas	7	A1
Fernside	17	C3
Ferry Lane	6	A2
Ferry Top Lane (Wintersett)	26	C3/35 A1
Ferrybridge Road (Castleford)	2	A2
Ferrybridge Road (Knottingley)	11	B1
Ferrybridge Road (Pontefract)	10	B2
Fewston Avenue	5	C3
Field Crescent	41	B1
Field Lane (Ossett)	13	B2
Field Lane (South Elmsall)	41	C2
Field Lane (Upton)	38	B3
Field Lane (Wakefield)	15	B3
Field Place	15	A2
Field View Cottages	19	A2
Field View	29	A3
Fieldhead Close	10	B3
Fieldhouse Street	16	A3
Fields End Court	38	B3
Fieldside Road	36	B1
Finch Avenue	25	A3
Finkin Avenue	5	C2
Finkin Croft	5	C2
Finkin Lane	5	C2
Finkle Close	32	C3
Finkle Street (Outwood)	32	C3
Finkle Street (Woolley)	10	A3
First Avenue (Fitzwilliam)	23	A1
First Avenue (Horbury)	5	B3
First Avenue (Newton Hill)	40	A3
First Avenue (South Kirkby)	38	B3
First Avenue (Upton)	28	A3
Firth Close	5	C1
Firthfield Lane	38	A1/30 A3
Firville Avenue	7	B3
Firville Crescent	7	B3
Fisher Grove	13	C2
Fisher Street	11	B1
Fishergate	11	A1
Fishpond Lane	24	B3
Fishponds Drive	24	B3
Fitzwilliam Street	36	C2
Flanshaw Avenue	14	C1
Flanshaw Crescent	14	C1
Flanshaw Grove	14	C1
Flanshaw Lane	14	B1
Flanshaw Road	14	C1
Flanshaw Street	14	C1
Flanshaw View	14	C1
Flanshaw Way	14	B1
Flass Lane	1	C3
Flavell Close	40	C3
Flounders Hill	28	C2
Foljambe Street	15	B2
Ford Street	36	C1
Forest Close	5	C3
Forester Close	36	B1
Forge Hill Lane	11	B1
Forge Lane	23 C1/24	A1
Forum View	30	B3
Foss Walk	2	C1
Foster Avenue	7	B3
Fothergill Avenue	28	C2
Foundry Lane	11	C1
Fountains Way	5	C3
Fourth Avenue	5	B3
Fox Court	24	B2
Fox Lane (Durkar)	24	B2
Fox Lane (Newton Bar)	5	A3
Fox Terrace	10	B3
Foxbridge Way	8	A2
Foxholes Lane	7	A1
Frain Close	20	A1
Francis Road	17	B3
Francis Street (Ackworth)	28	B3
Francis Street (Castleford)	2	A1
Francis Terrace	28	B3
Frederick Avenue	16	A3
Frederick Street	15	B1
Frederick Street	T/C	D2
Freeston Court	7	B2
Freeston Drive (Normanton)	7	B2
Freestone Avenue	16	C1
Freestone Drive	16	C1
Freestone Way (Altofts)	6	C2
Freestone Way (Kirkthorpe)	16	C1
Frensham Drive	3	A2
Friar's Close	19	A2
Friars Nook	20	B1
Friarwood Lane	10	A3
Friarwood Steps	20	A1
Friarwood Terrace	10	A3
Frickley Lane	41	C3
Frobisher Grove	14	C2
Front Street (Glass Houghton)	2	B3
Front Street (Pontefract)	9	C3
Fryergate	14	C1
Fryston Lane	3	B2
Fryston Road	2 C2/3	A1
Fulford Street	1	C2
Fulmar Road	1	C2
Fulwood Grove	24	C3
Furlong Lane	20	B2
Furness Avenue	4	C3
Furness Drive	4	C3

G

Street	Map	Grid
Gabriel's Corner	28	C3
Gagewell Drive	14	A3
Gagewell Lane	14	A3
Gagewell View	14	A3
Gainsborough Way	5	C1
Gallon Croft	41	A2
Gallows Hill	3	A2
Gallows Lane	32	C2
Gannet Close	1	C3
Garden Close	13	B3
Garden Lane	11	C1
Garden Row	26	C1
Garden Street (Ackworth)	28	B3
Garden Street (Altofts)	7	A2
Garden Street (Castleford)	2	A2
Garden Street (Glass Houghton)	2	B3
Garden Street (Normanton)	7	B3
Garden Street (Wakefield)	15	B2
Garden Street	T/C	C2
Garden Terrace (Painthorpe)	24	A3
Garden Terrace (Ryhill)	35	B2
Garforth Close	6	C2
Garforth Drive	6	C2
Gargrave Crescent	36	C3
Gargrave Place (Hemsworth)	36	C3
Gargrave Place (Wakefield)	14	B2
Garmil Head Lane	27	C3
Garmil Lane	27	C2
Garsdale Grove	5 C3/6	A3
Garsdale Walk	11	B2
Garth Avenue	7	B3
Garth Cottages	12	A2
Garth Street	1	C3
Gaskell Drive	13	C3
Gaskell Street	T/C	A3
Gateways	5	B1
Gawthorpe Lane	4	A3
Geary Close	4	B3
Geary Drive	4	B3
Gelder Court	4	B3
Gelder Croft	4	B3
Gemini Court	10	A2
Geneva Grove	15	B1
Geneva Grove	T/C	D1
George & Crown Yard	T/C	C2
George Buckley Court	40	B2
George Lane	33	C3
George Street (Altofts)	7	A2
George Street (Featherstone)	18	C2
George Street (Horbury)	23	C1
George Street (Ossett)	13	A1
George Street (Outwood)	5	B1
George Street (Ryhill)	35	B1
George Street (South Hiendley)	35	C3
George Street (Streethouse)	17	C2

Street	Page	Grid
George Street (Wakefield)	15	B2
George Street	T/C	D3
George-A-Green Road	14	C2
George And Crown Yard	15	B1
Georgia Mews	13	C2
Gervase Road	23	B1
Gibson Avenue	14	C1
Gibson Close	15	A1
Gilcar Street	7	C2
Gill Sike Avenue	14	C3
Gill Sike Bungalows	14	C3
Gill Sike Grove	14	C2
Gill Sike Road	14	C2
Gill Street	T/C	C2
Gillann Street	11	C2
Gillion Crescent	24	A3
Gills Yard	15	B1
Gills Yard	T/C	C1
Gillygate	10	A3
Gin Lane	17	C2
Gipsy Lane (Sandal)	25	B2
Gipsy Lane (Woolley)	32	C3
Girnhill Lane	18	C3
Gisburn Road	6	A3
Gissing Road	14	B2
Gladstone Street (Featherstone)	19	A1
Gladstone Street (Normanton)	7	C2
Gladstone Terrace	2	A1
Glastonbury Avenue	6	A3
Glebe Lane	11	C1
Glebe Street (Castleford)	2	A2
Glebe Street (Normanton)	7	C3
Glendale	23	A1
Gleneagles Road	9	A3
Glenfields Close	23	A3
Glenfields	23	A3
Glenholme Terrace	13	A1
Gloucester Grove	14	B2
Gloucester Place	14	B2
Gloucester Road	14	B2
Golden Square	23	B1
Good Hope Close	7	C2
Goosehill Lane	16	C1
Goosehill Road	7	A3
Goosehole Lane	41	C3
Gordon Avenue	13	B2
Gordon Place	41	B3
Gordon Street (Featherstone)	19	A1
Gordon Street (Wakefield)	15	C3
Gordon Terrace	11	C2
Goring Park Avenue	14	A2
Gorton Street	36	C2
Gothic Mount	8	B3
Governor's Yard	T/C	E1
Grafton Close	11	B1
Grafton Street	2	A3
Graham Avenue	39	A2
Graham Drive	2	C2
Grampian Avenue	14	C3
Granby Court	41	B1
Grandstand Road	4	C1
Grange Avenue	41	B2
Grange Close (Badsworth)	38	A1
Grange Close (Knottingley)	11	B1
Grange Cottages	10	B2
Grange Court	38	A1
Grange Drive	13	C3
Grange Lane	22	A3
Grange Rise	36	C3
Grange Road	3	A1
Grange Street	15	A2
Grange Street	T/C	A3
Grange View	37	A3
Grangeway	36	C3
Grangewood Court	5	B2
Grantley Street	15	B1
Grantley Street	T/C	E2
Grantley Way	15	C1
Grantley Way	T/C	E1
Granville Avenue (Normanton)	10	A3
Granville Street (Cutsyke)	1	C3
Granville Street (Featherstone)	18	C2
Granville Street (Normanton)	7	B3
Grasmere Close	3	B1
Grasmere Road (Alverthorpe)	14	C1
Grasmere Road (Knottingley)	11	B2
Great North Road	30 C1/39	C1
Greatfield Close	13	B2
Greatfield Court	13	B2
Greatfield Drive	13	B2
Greatfield Gardens	13	B2
Greatfield Road	13	B2
Greavefield Lane	10	C3
Greaves Avenue	14	B2
Greaves Street	2	A2
Greaves Yard	23	B1
Greek Street	2	A1
Green Croft	36	B1
Green End Lane	15	B3
Green Lane (Ackworth)	28	B3
Green Lane (Alverthorpe)	14	B1
Green Lane (Carleton)	20	B2
Green Lane (Castleford)	2	B1
Green Lane (Cutsyke)	1	C3
Green Lane (Featherstone)	18 B1/B2/19	A1
Green Lane (Horbury)	23	C1
Green Lane (Kirkthorpe)	16	B1
Green Lane (Middlestown)	22	A2
Green Lane (Netherton)	23 A3/24	A1
Green Lane (Notton)	34	A3
Green Lane (Pontefract)	20	A1
Green Lane (South Kirkby)	40	B2
Green Lane (Upton)	38	C2
Green Lane Close	22	A2
Green Park Avenue (Hall Cliff)	13	C3
Green Park Avenue (South Ossett)	13	B3
Green Park Avenue	23	B1
Green Park	15	C1
Green Park	T/C	F2
Green Side	25	C2
Green Street	2	A1
Green, The (Castleford)	3	A1
Green, The (Featherstone)	19	A3
Green, The (Normanton)	7	B3
Green, The (Notton)	34	A3
Green, The (Ossett)	13	B2
Green, The (Sharlston)	17	C3
Green, The (South Kirkby)	41	A2
Green, The (Woolley)	33	A3
Green, The (Wrenthorpe)	4	C2
Green Acres (Durkar)	24	B2
Green Acres (Gawthorpe)	13	B1
Green Acres (Featherstone)	19	A3
Greenacre Road	38	C2
Greenacre Walk	35	C1
Greenacres	13	B1
Greenacres Close	13	B1
Greenbank Grove	7	A2
Greenbank Road	7	A2
Greenfield Avenue	13	C3
Greenfield Close (Ossett)	13	C3
Greenfield Close (Wrenthorpe)	4	C3
Greenfield Mount	4	C3
Greenfield Road (Altofts)	7	A3
Greenfield Road (Hemsworth)	36	C3
Greenfield Road (Ossett)	13	C3
Greenfield Way	4	C3
Greenhill Avenue	20	B1
Greenhill Mount	20	B1
Greenhill Road	15	C1
Greenhill Road	T/C	E1
Greenlay Drive	4	A3
Greenroyd Court	21	A2
Greenside (Featherstone)	19	A1
Greenside (Ryhill)	35	B2
Greenside Court	27	A2
Greenside Park	27	A2
Greentop	27	A2
Greenview	27	A2
Greenwood Avenue	38	C2
Greenwood Close (Featherstone)	17	B1
Greenwood Close (Upton)	38	C2
Greenwood Road	15	C1
Greenwood Road	T/C	E1
Gregory Road	2	B3
Greigs Yard	23	A1
Grenley Street	11	C1
Grenville Walk	32	C1
Grey Close	5	B2
Grey Court	5	B2
Grey Gables	23	A2
Grey Street	5	B2
Greystones Drive	13	B3
Grime Lane	17	B3
Grimethorpe Street	41	B2
Grosvenor Avenue (Pontefract)	9	C3
Grosvenor Avenue (Upton)	38	B3
Grosvenor Street	16	A3
Grove Avenue (Hemsworth)	37	A3
Grove Avenue (Pontefract)	10	B3
Grove Avenue (South Kirkby)	40	C2
Grove Crescent (Walton)	25	C2
Grove Drive	40	B2
Grove Head	40	C3
Grove Lane (Badsworth)	38	A1
Grove Lane (Hemsworth)	37	A3
Grove Lane (Knottingley)	11	B1
Grove Lane (South Kirkby)	40	C2
Grove Lea Close	37	A3
Grove Lea Crescent	20	A1
Grove Lea Walk	20	B1
Grove Mount (Pontefract)	10	B3
Grove Mount (South Kirkby)	40	C2
Grove Park	24	A2
Grove Place	37	A3
Grove Rise	10	B3
Grove Road (Horbury)	23	B1
Grove Road (Pontefract)	20	A1/B1
Grove Road (Wakefield)	15	B2
Grove Road	T/C	D3
Grove Street (Ossett)	13	B3
Grove Street (South Kirkby)	40	C2
Grove Street (Wakefield)	15	B2
Grove Street	T/C	D3
Grove Terrace	37	A3
Grove Way	40	C2
Grove, The (Normanton)	7	B3
Grove, The (Ryhill)	35	B2
Grove, The (South Elmsall)	41	B2
Grove, The (Walton)	25	C2
Grovehall Lane	10	C3
Grovehall Lane	11	A3
Guildford Road	34	B3
Guildford Street	13	B3
Gunson Crescent	13	B2
Guys Croft	14	B2
Gypsy Court (Castleford)	3	A2
Gypsy Lane	3	A2/A3

H

Street	Page	Grid
Hacking Lane	41	C2
Haddon Close	41	B1
Hadleigh Rise	19	C2
Hadrian Close (Castleford)	3	A1
Hadrian Close (Thorpe Audlin)	30	A3
Haggs Hill Road	13	C2
Haggs Lane	14	A2
Hague Crescent	37	A3
Hague Lane	40	A3
Hague Terrace	37	A3
Haigh Hill Lane	32	B3
Haigh Moor Street	15	B1
Hailhead Drive	10	B3
Halberg House	10 B3/20	B1
Haldane Crescent	5 C3/6	A3
Half Moon Lane	16	B1
Halfpenny Lane (Featherstone)	19	B1
Halfpenny Lane (Pontefract)	9	C3
Hall Cliffe Crescent	14	A3
Hall Cliffe Grove	14	A3
Hall Cliffe Rise	14	A3
Hall Cliffe Road	14	A3
Hall Close (Gawthorpe)	13	A1
Hall Close (Hemsworth)	37	A3
Hall Croft	23	A2
Hall Field Lane	35	A2
Hall Garth Road	30	A3
Hall Lane (Chapelthorpe)	24	A2
Hall Lane (North Elmsall)	38	C3
Hall Park Avenue	26 C1/17	A3
Hall Rise	37	A3
Hall Road	14	B2
Hall Street	19	A2
Hallamshire Mews	14	B2
Hallcroft Close	23	C1
Hallcroft Drive	23	C1
Hallcroft Grange	7	B3
Halton Road	5	C3
Halton Street	19	A1
Hambleton Street	T/C	D1
Hamel Rise	37	A3
Hamilton Court	7	B2
Hammer Lane	17	B3
Hammond Road	11	B2
Hampden Close	3	C3
Hanby Avenue	7	A2
Handsworth Road	24	B3
Hanover Court	23	B1
Hanover Crescent	19	C2
Hanover Street	15	A2
Hanover Street	T/C	A3
Hanson Avenue	7	A3
Hanson House	7	B3
Hardaker's Lane	28	C3
Hardakers Approach	28	C3
Hardcastle Avenue	10	A3
Hardcastle Lane	22	A3
Hardie Road	35	C2
Hardisty Drive	9	C3
Hardwick Court	20	A1
Hardwick Crescent	20	A2
Hardwick Lane	28	A1
Hardwick Road (East Hardwick)	20	B3
Hardwick Road (Featherstone)	18	C2
Hardwick Road (Pontefract)	20	A2/A3
Hardy Croft	15	B2
Hardy Croft	T/C	E2
Hare Park Lane	26	C2
Hare Park View	26	C1
Harefield Road	10	B3
Harewood Avenue (Normanton)	7	C2
Harewood Avenue (Pontefract)	10 B3/20	B1
Harewood Close	11	A1
Harewood Lane	39	B1
Harewood Mount	10	B3
Harewood Road	5 C3/6	A3
Harewood View	10	B3
Hargreaves Avenue	5	C1
Hargreaves Yard	23	B1
Harker Street	12	A1
Harlock Street	15	C3
Harrap Street	14	B1
Harrison Road	26	C1
Harrop Well Lane	10	A3
Harrow Street	41	A2
Hartley Close	41	B1
Hartley Park Avenue	9	C3
Hartley Park View	9	C3
Hartley Street	1	C2
Hartley Terrace	18	C2
Harvey Street	15	C3
Harwood Close	25	B1
Harewood Drive	4	B3
Haselden Crescent	14	B2
Haselden Road	14	B2
Haste Street	1	C1
Hastings Avenue	15	B3
Hastings Court	6	C2
Hastings Crescent	2	C1
Hastings Grove	15	B3
Hastings Walk	2	C2
Hatfeild Street	15	B1
Hatfeild Street	T/C	D1
Hatfield Place	35	C1
Haven Court	19	C2
Havercroft Green	35	B2
Havercroft Lane	21	B2
Havercroft Rise	36	A3
Havercroft	13	C2
Haverdale Road	35	C2
Haveroid Lane	24	B3
Haveroid Way	24	B3
Havertop Lane	8	A2
Haw Hill View	7	B2
Haw Park Lane	35	A1
Hawes Close	2	C1
Haweswater Place	11	B3
Hawkingcroft Road	23	A1
Hawthorn Avenue (Crofton)	26	B1
Hawthorn Avenue (Knottingley)	11	B2
Hawthorn Close	4	A2

Street	Page	Grid
Hawthorn Court	26	B1
Hawthorn Grove	29	A3
Hawthorn Terrace	13	B3
Hawthorne Avenue (Castleford)	2	C2
Hawthorne Avenue (Featherstone)	18	C3
Hawthorne Avenue (Hemsworth)	36	C3
Hawthorne Crescent	36	C3
Hawthorne Grove	14	C1
Hawthorne Mount	17	B1
Hawthorne Terrace	14	C1
Hawthorns, The (Ossett)	13	B3
Hawthorns, The (Outwood)	5	B1
Haydn Avenue	5	C1
Hayne Lane	22	A3
Hazel Court	15	A1
Hazel Gardens	3	A3
Hazel Garth	11	B2
Hazel Road	11	B2
Hazelwood Court	5	C2
Hazelwood Road (Kinsley)	36	C2
Hazelwood Road (Outwood)	5	B1
Headlands Avenue	13	A2
Headlands Grove	13	A2
Headlands Lane (Knottingley)	11	B1
Headlands Lane (Pontefract)	10	A3
Headlands Park	13	A2
Headlands Road (Ossett)	13	A2
Headlands Road (Pontefract)	10	A3
Headlands Villas	10	A3
Headlands Walk	13	A2
Heald Street	2	B1
Healdfield Road	2	B1
Healdwood Close	2	B1
Healdwood Road	2	B1
Healey Crescent	13	B3
Healey Drive	13	B3
Healey Road	13	B3
Healey View	13	B3
Heath Hall	16	B2
Heather Close (Ossett)	13	C3
Heather Close (South Kirkby)	41	C2
Heather Close (Stanley)	5	C1
Heather Court	5	C1
Heather View	13	B2
Heathfield Road	13	A1
Heaton Street	28	C3
Hebden Road	5	C3
Hedley Crescent	5	A2
Heeley Road	24	C3
Hell Lane	16	C2
Hellewells Row	23	A1
Helmsley Road	25	B1
Helston Road	7	B2
Hemsby Road	1	C2
Hemsworth By-Pass	36/37	
Hemsworth Lane	27	C3
Hemsworth Road	37	A3
Hendal Lane	24	B3
Henderson Avenue	7	B3
Henley Drive	19	A3
Henry Avenue	35	C2
Henry Moore Place	2	A2
Henry Street	15	A1
Henry Street	T/C	
Henson Grove	2	C2
Hepworth Street	2	B1
Herbert Street	1	C2
Hereford Close	37	A2
Heron Drive	25	A3
Heseltine Close	7	A3
Hesley Road	24	C3
Hessle Common Lane	28	B2
Hessle Lane	28	C1
Heys Buildings	7	A2
High Close	13	A1
High Farm Fold	38	B1
High Farm Meadow	38	B1
High Green Road	6	C2
High Meadows	25	C2
High Oxford Street	1	C2
High Ridge	23	A2
High Street (Altofts)	7	A2
High Street (Crigglestone)	24	A3
High Street (Crofton)	26	C1
High Street (Ferrybridge)	11	A1
High Street (Gawthorpe)	13	A1
High Street (Hemsworth)	37	A3
High Street (Horbury)	23	B1
High Street (New Sharlston)	17	A2
High Street (Normanton)	7	B3
High Street (South Elmsall)	41	C2
High Street (South Hiendley)	36	A3
High Street (Upton)	38	C3
High Street (Woolley)	33	A3
High View	24	A3
High Well Hill Lane	35	C3
High Well Lane	35	C2
High Ash Close	34	A3
Highfield Avenue	3	C3
Highfield Close	9	A3
Highfield Court	1	C2
Highfield Crescent (Hemsworth)	36	C3
Highfield Crescent (Middlestown)	22	A2
Highfield Drive	14	C1
Highfield Grange	23	B1
Highfield Lane	36	C3
Highfield Place (Hemsworth)	36	C3
Highfield Place (Horbury)	23	B1
Highfield Rise	14	C1
Highfield Road (Hemsworth)	36	C3
Highfield Road (Horbury)	23	B1
Highfield Road (Netherton)	22	C3
Highfield Road (Pontefract)	20	A1
Highfields (Havercroft)	35	C1
Highfields (Netherton)	22	C3
Highland Close	10	B2
Highlands, The	13	A2
Hilda Street	13	B3
Hill Close	20	A1
Hill Crest	35	C2
Hill Croft Close	21	A2
Hill Drive	29	A1
Hill Estate	38	C3
Hill Road (Castleford)	2	B2
Hill Road (Newmillerdam)	25	A3
Hill Thorpe Drive	30	B3
Hill Top (Castleford)	1	A2
Hill Top (Fitzwilliam)	36	B1
Hill Top (Knottingley)	11	B1
Hill Top (Pledwick)	25	A3
Hill Top Close (Notton)	34	B3
Hill Top Close (Fitzwilliam)	36	B1
Hill Top Court	25	A3
Hill Top Estate	40	B3
Hill Top Lane	28	B1
Hill Top Mews	11	B1
Hill Top Road	25	A3
Hill Top View	17	B1
Hillcrest Avenue (Castleford)	3	A2
Hillcrest Avenue (Featherstone)	18	C2
Hillcrest Avenue (Gawthorpe)	13	A1
Hillcrest Close	3	A2
Hillcrest Drive	3	A2
Hillcrest Mount	3	A2
Hillcrest Road	3	B2
Hillcrest	7	A2
Hillfold	41	C2
Hillgarth	11	B2
Hillsboro Villas	41	B3
Hillside Close	14	B3
Hillside Court	41	B1
Hillside Mount	10	B3
Hillside Road (Ackworth)	29	A3
Hillside Road (Pontefract)	10	B3
Hilmian Way	37	A3
Hinchcliffe Avenue	13	C2
Hinchcliffe Houses	41	C2
Hinds Crescent	41	B2
Hinton Lane	3	C2/C3
Hirst Road	14	B2
Hirstlands Avenue	13	A1
Hirstlands Drive	13	A1
Hob Lane	40	B2
Hobart Road	3	A1
Hodgewood Lane	21	B1
Hodgson Street	15	A1
Hodgson Street	T/C	B1
Holby Square	14	B2
Holderness Road	11	B1
Holes Lane	11	B1
Holgate Avenue	36	B1
Holgate Crescent	36	C3
Holgate Gardens	36	C3
Holgate Road	19	C2
Holgate Terrace	36	B1
Holgate View	36	B1
Hollin Drive	24	A3
Hollin Lane	24	A2
Hollingthorpe Avenue	32	C1
Hollingthorpe Court	32	C1
Hollingthorpe Grove	32	C1
Hollingthorpe Lane	32	C1
Hollingthorpe Road	32	C1
Hollingworth Lane	11	C1
Hollinhirst Lane	23	A3
Hollins Mount	36	C3
Highland Close	10	B2
Holly Approach	13	B1
Holly Close (Crofton)	26	B1
Holly Close (South Elmsall)	41	B3
Holly Court	5	B1
Holly Crescent	26	B1
Holly Dene	13	B1
Holly Mede	13	B1
Holly Street (Hemsworth)	37	A2
Holly Street (Wakefield)	14	C1
Hollybank	28	C2
Holme Croft	24	B2
Holme Field	13	A1
Holme Lane	15	A3
Holme Leas Drive	13	A1
Holme Way	13	A1
Holmefield Avenue	15	B3
Holmefield Grove	15	B3
Holmefield Lane	15	B3
Holmfield Chase	6	B1
Holmfield Close	10	B2
Holmfield Cottages	3	B2
Holmfield Lane	3	B3
Holmsley Avenue	40	B2
Holmsley Grove	40	B2
Holmsley Lane	40	A3
Holmsley Mount	40	B2
Holt's Yard	T/C	C2
Holyoake Terrace	23	A1
Holyrood Crescent	7	A2
Holywell Dene	2	B3
Holywell Gardens	2	B3
Holywell Grove	2	B3
Holywell Lane	2	B3/C2
Holywell Mount	2	C2
Home Farm Court	31	C3
Home Farm	33	A3
Homestead Drive	14	C1
Honley House	23	B1
Honley Square	23	B1
Hood Street	41	B3
Hooton Crescent	35	B2
Hope Street (Normanton)	7	B3
Hope Street (Ossett)	13	C3
Hope Street (Ryhill)	35	C2
Hope Street (Wakefield)	T/C	D1
Hope Street East	2	A2
Hope Terrace (Crofton)	26	C1
Hope Terrace (Pontefract)	9	C3
Hopetown Walk	7	C2
Hopewell Way	24	A3
Hopwood Grove	2	C2
Horbury Mews	23	A1
Horbury Road (Ossett)	13	B3
Horbury Road (Wakefield)	14	B3/C3
Horbury Road	T/C	A3
Hornbeam Avenue	15	A1
Hornbeam Green	10	B3
Horncastle View (Fitzwilliam)	36	A1
Horncastle View (Havercroft)	35	C1
Horne Street	15	B2
Horse Fair Flats	10	A3
Horse Fair	10	A3
Horton Street	13	A2
Hostingley Lane	22	C1
Houghton Avenue	11	A1
Houndhill Lane	19	B2
Howard Crescent	24	A3
Howard Street (Ossett)	13	B2
Howard Street (Wakefield)	15	B1
Howard Street	T/C	C1
Howden Way	15	C1
Howden Way	T/C	F3
Howroyds Yard	13	A1
Hoyland Road	24	C3
Hoyland Terrace	40	B2
Hoyle Mill Road	36	C2/37 A1
Huddersfield Road	31	B2
Hudson Avenue	34	B3
Hudswell Street	15	C3
Hugh Street	2	A2
Hulme Square	3	A1
Humber Close	2	C1
Humber Place	23	B1
Humley Road	24	C3
Hundhill Lane	20	A3/29 B1
Hunt Court	14	B1
Hunt Street (Castleford)	2	A1
Hunt Street (Whitwood Mere)	1	C2
Huntsman Fold	14	B1
Huntsman's Way	38	A1
Huntwick Avenue	18	C2
Huntwick Crescent	18	C3
Huntwick Drive	18	C2
Huntwick Lane	18	B2
Huntwick Road	18	C3
Hutton Drive	41	B1
Hyde Park	15	C1
Hyde Park	T/C	F2
Hyman Walk	41	B1

I

Street	Page	Grid
Ibbottson Street	16	A3
Illingworth Avenue	7	A2
Illingworth Street	13	B2
Imperial Avenue	4	C2
Industrial Street (Horbury)	23	C1
Industrial Street (Wakefield)	15	B1
Industrial Street	T/C	D1
Ingfield Avenue	13	B2
Ingram Crescent	11	A2
Ings Close (Havercroft)	35	C1
Ings Close (Moorthorpe)	41	C2
Ings Holt	41	A2
Ings House	36	B3
Ings Lane	2	B1
Ings Road (Kinsley)	36	C2
Ings Road (Wakefield)	15	A2
Ings Road	T/C	B3
Ings View	2	C1
Ings Walk	41	A2
Ingswell Avenue	34	A3
Ingswell Drive	34	A3
Ingwell Street	15	B2
Ingwell Street	T/C	E3
Intake Close	6	A2
Intake Lane (Ossett)	13	B2
Intake Lane (Stanley)	6	A1
Intake Lane (Woolley)	32	C2
Irwin Avenue	15	C1
Irwin Crescent	15	C1
Island, The	11	C1
Ivy Close (South Elmsall)	41	B3
Ivy Close (Wakefield)	5	C3
Ivy Gardens	3	A3
Ivy Grange	34	A3
Ivy Grove	15	C1
Ivy Lane	5 C3/15 C1	
Ivy Street	19	A1
Ivy Terrace (Horbury)	23	B1
Ivy Terrace (South Elmsall)	41	B2

J

Street	Page	Grid
Jackson's Lane	30	C2
Jacksons Court	10	A3
Jacob's Well Lane	15	B1
Jacob's Well Lane	T/C	D1
Jaglin Court	19	A2
James Duggan Avenue	18	C2
James Gibbs Close	19	B2
James Street (Castleford)	2	A1
James Street (South Hiendley)	36	A3
Jardine Avenue	19	A1
Jenkin Drive	23	B1
Jenkin Lane	23	A1
Jenkin Road	23	B1
Jerry Clay Drive	4	C3

Street	Page	Grid
Jerry Clay Lane	4	B2
Jessop Street (Castleford)	2	A2
Jessop Street (Thornes)	15	B3
Jin Whin Hill	1	B2
Jin Whin Terrace	1	B2
Joffre Avenue	2	A2
John Carr Avenue	13	C3
John Street (Castleford)	1	C2
John Street (South Elmsall)	41	B2
John Street (Wakefield)	15	C2
John Street	T/C	E2
John's Crescent	4	C3
Johns Avenue	5	B1
Johnston Street	15	C1
Johnston Street	T/C	E2
Jons Avenue	40	B2
Jubbs Yard	23	B1
Jubilee Avenue (Normanton)	7	B3
Jubilee Avenue (Outwood)	5	B2
Jubilee Bungalows	11	B1
Jubilee Close	37	B3
Jubilee Cottages	35	B2
Jubilee Crescent (Outwood)	5	B2
Jubilee Crescent (Sharlston)	17	B3
Jubilee Place	10	A3
Jubilee Road	17	B3
Jubilee Street	32	C1
Jubilee Terrace	29	A1
Jubilee Way	10	A3
Julie Avenue	24	A3
Junction Lane	13	C2
Junction Street	37	A3

K

Street	Page	Grid
Karon Drive	23	B1
Katrina Grove	19	A3
Kay Street	15	C2
Kay Street	T/C	E2
Keats Close	10	A2
Keats Grove	5	C1
Keenan Avenue	41	B3
Keeper Lane	33	C3
Kemp's Bridge	15	A2
Kemp's Bridge	T/C	A3
Ken Churchill Drive	13	C3
Kendal Close	3	A2
Kendal Croft	3	B2
Kendal Drive (Castleford)	3	A1/A2
Kendal Drive (Crofton)	16	B3
Kendal Drive	25	C2
Kendal Gardens	3	A2
Kendal Garth	3	A2
Kendal Hall Close	25	B1
Kendal Rise	16	B3
Kenmore Road	4	C2
Kensington Road	5	B3
Kenton Drive	24	B2
Kenyon Street	41	B2
Keren Grove	4	C3
Kershaw Avenue	2	C2
Kershaw Lane	11	B2
Kestrel Drive	25	A3
Keswick Drive (Alverthorpe)	14	C1
Keswick Drive (Castleford)	3	A1
Kettlethorpe Hall Drive	25	A2
Kettlethorpe Road	24	C3
Kilby Street	15	A1
Kilnsey Grove	15	C1
Kilnsey Road	15	C1
Kimberley Street (Featherstone)	18	C1
Kimberley Street (Wakefield)	15	C3
Kimberly Close	30	B3
King Edward Street (Hemsworth)	37	A3
King Edward Street (Normanton)	7	B3
King George Street	5	A2
King Royd Lane	28	B2
King Street (Altofts)	7	A2
King Street (Glass Houghton)	2	A3
King Street (Horbury)	23	A1
King Street (Kinsley)	36	C1
King Street (Moorthorpe)	41	B2
King Street (Normanton)	7	A2
King Street (Ossett)	13	C3
King Street (Pontefract)	9	C3
King Street (Wakefield)	15	B1
King Street	T/C	C2
King's Crescent	20	B1
Kingfisher Close	24	B2
Kingfisher Grove	25	A3
Kings Avenue (Airedale)	2	C2
Kings Avenue (Altofts)	7	A1
Kings Close (Ackworth)	28	C3
Kings Close (Ossett)	13	A1
Kings Close (Pontefract)	20	A1
Kings Court	36	C2
Kings Croft (Ossett)	13	A1
Kings Croft (South Kirkby)	40	C2
Kings Drive	7	A1
Kings Lea	13	A1
Kings Mead	19	C1
Kings Meadow	13	A1
Kings Mount	11	A1
Kings Paddock	13	A1
Kings Road	7	A1
Kings Villas	11	B1
Kings Yard	23	A1
Kingsley Avenue (Crofton)	17	A3
Kingsley Avenue (Featherstone)	19	A1
Kingsley Avenue (Knottingley)	11	A1
Kingsley Avenue (Outwood)	5	A1
Kingsley Avenue (Sandal)	25	A2
Kingsley Close (Crofton)	17	A3
Kingsley Close (Sandal)	25	A2
Kingsley Close (Outwood)	5	A1
Kingsley Garth	5	A1
Kingsmead	13	A1
Kingsway (Ossett)	13	A1
Kingsway (Pontefract)	10	A2
Kingsway	6	A2
Kingsway (Woodhouse)	17	B1
Kingsway Close	13	A1
Kingsway Court	13	A1
Kingswell Avenue	5	B2
Kinsley House Crescent	36	B1
Kinsley Street	36	B2
Kipling Grove	10	A2
Kirkbridge Way	41	B2
Kirkby Close	40	C2
Kirkby Road	37	A3
Kirkbygate Lane	37	A3
Kirkbygate	37	A3
Kirkdale Drive	24	A3
Kirkdale	2	C2
Kirkgate	15	B2
Kirkgate	T/C	D2
Kirkgate Lane	35	C3
Kirkham Avenue	4	A2
Kirkhaw Lane	3	C2
Kirkthorpe Lane	16	B1
Knightscroft Parade	41	B2
Knightsway	25	A2
Knoll Close	13	B2
Knottingley Road (Pontefract)	10	B2
Knottingley Road (Ferrybridge)	11	A2
Knowles Walk	41	B1

L

Street	Page	Grid
Laburnum Court (Castleford)	2	A2
Laburnum Court (Horbury)	23	B1
Laburnum Grove	23	B1
Laburnum Road	15	B1
Laburnum Road	T/C	C1
Lacey Street	14	B3
Lacy Street	36	C3
Lady Balk Lane	10	A2
Lady Close	13	A1
Lady Lane	15	B2
Lady Lane	T/C	C3
Lafflands Lane	35	B2
Laithes Court	14	B1
Laithes Drive	14	B1
Laithes View	14	B1
Lake Court	24	C3
Lake Ends View	5	C1
Lake Lock Drive	6	A1
Lake Lock Grove	6	A1
Lake Lock Road	6	A1
Lake View (Pontefract)	10	A2
Lake View (Newmillerdam)	24	C3
Lake View Flats	24	C3
Lake Yard	6	A1
Lakeland Way	25	C2
Lakeside Estate	35	B1
Lamb Inn Road	11	C1
Lanark Rise	26	C1
Lancaster Close	20	A1
Lancaster Street	3	A1
Lands Buildings	13	B1
Landsdown Avenue	40	B3
Lane Ends Close	27	C3
Langdale Avenue (Altofts)	7	A2
Langdale Avenue (Outwood)	5	B1
Langdale Close	3	B1
Langdale Drive (Ackworth)	29	B2
Langdale Drive (Altofts)	7	A2
Langdale Drive (Wakefield)	14	C1
Langdale Mews	7	B2
Langdale Mount	25	C2
Langdale Square	14	C1
Langsett Road	24	C3
Langthwaite Lane	41	A3
Langthwaite Road	41	A2
Lansdowne Avenue	2	B2
Larch Close	7	B3
Larch Court	2	A2
Larks Hill	19	C1
Laurel Court	13	A2
Lawefield Grove	15	A2
Lawefield Grove	T/C	A3
Lawefield Lane	15	A2
Lawefield Lane	T/C	A3
Lawns Close	7	A2
Lawns Court	4	C1
Lawns Lane	4	C1
Lawns View	6	C2
Lawns, The	22	B2
Laythorpe Court	20	C1
Lea Lane	19	A2
Leaf Street	1	C2
Leake Street	2	A2
Leatham Avenue	19	A2
Leatham Crescent	19	B2
Leatham Drive	19	B2
Leatham Park Road	19	B2
Ledgard Drive	24	B2
Ledger Lane	5	A2
Ledger Place	5	A2
Lee Brig	7	A2
Lee Court	13	C3
Lee Lane	29	A1
Lee Moor Road	5	C1
Lee Street	T/C	C2
Leeds Road (Castleford)	1	C1
Leeds Road (Cutsyke)	2	A3
Leeds Road (Gawthorpe)	13	A1
Leeds Road (Outwood)	5	B1
Leeke Avenue	13	C3
Lees Crescent	24	B2
Leigh Street	28	B3
Lemon Tree Close	19	C1
Lennox Drive	14	B3
Leopold Street	14	A2
Lewin Grove	3	A1
Leybrook Croft	37	A2
Leyland Road	3	A1
Leys Lane	11	C2
Leys Road	21	B2
Leys, The	40	C2
Lidgate Crescent	41	A2
Lidget Lane (Sharlston)	17 C3/27	B1
Light Lane	14	C1
Lightfoot Avenue	2	A3
Lightfoot Close	2	A3
Lilac Avenue (Knottingley)	11	B2
Lilac Avenue (Wakefield)	15	B3
Lilac Cottages	20	B2
Lilley Street	37	A3
Lilley Terrace	40	C2
Lilygarth	11	A1
Lime Crescent (Sandal)	25	B1
Lime Crescent (South Elmsall)	41	A3
Lime Grove	41	A3
Lime Pit Lane	5 C2/6	A1
Lime Street	13	B3
Lime Tree Avenue	19	C1
Lime Tree Court	36	C3
Limetrees	3	C3
Lincoln Crescent	41	C1
Lincoln Street (Castleford)	2	A1
Lincoln Street (Wakefield)	14	C1
Lincoln Street	T/C	A1
Lindale Avenue	29	C3
Lindale Garth	4	A2
Lindale Grove	4	B3
Lindale Lane	4	B3
Lindale Mount	4	B3
Linden Close (Knottingley)	11	A1
Linden Close (Townville)	3	A2
Linden Street	28	B3
Linden Terrace	9	C3
Lindsay Avenue	14	B2
Lings Lane	39	B2
Lingwell Chase	5	B1
Lingwell Court	5	A1
Lingwell Gate Crescent	5	A1
Lingwell Gate Drive	5	A1
Lingwell Gate Lane	5	A1
Lingwell Nook Lane	5	B1
Link Road	5	A3
Link, The	19	C1
Links, The	9	A3
Linnet Grove	25	A3
Linton Road	16	A1
Lionel Street	13	B3
Liquorice Way	10	A3
Lisheen Avenue	2	A2
Lisheen Green	2	A2
Lister Close	18	C2
Lister Road	18	C2
Lister Street	1	C2
Litell Royd	17	C2
Little Hemsworth	37	A3
Little Lane (Featherstone)	19	A2
Little Lane (Upton)	38	C3
Little Lane (South Elmsall)	41	B2/C2
Little Went Bridge	19	A3
Little Westgate	T/C	C2/D2
Littlefield Grove	13	B2
Littlefield Road	13	B2
Littlejohn Crescent	14	C3
Litton Croft	16	A1
Lock Lane (Altofts)	7	A1
Lock Lane (Castleford)	2	A1
Lodge Avenue	3	A2
Lodge Farm Gardens	7	A2
Lodge Hill Road	13	A1
Lodge Lane (Crofton)	16 C3/26	B1
Lodge Lane (Pledwick)	25	B3
Lodge Street	37	B2
Lodges Close	35	C1
Lombardi Court	13	C2
Lombardy Garth	5	A3
Long Causeway	5	C1/B3
Long Close Lane	38	C3
Long Crest	20	B1
Long Dam Lane	26 C3/35	B1
Long Lane (Carleton)	20	B1
Long Lane (Ackworth)	29	B1
Long Lane Close	29	B1
Long Row	17	A2
Longacre	2	A2
Longdale Drive	41	A2
Longfellow Grove	5	C1
Longfield Drive	29	B2
Longfield Terrace	14	C1
Longlands Close	13	B2
Longlands Road	13	B2
Longwoods Walk	11	C1
Lonsborough Way	41	C1
Lonsdale Road	5	A3
Lord Street	15	C3
Lorna Cottages	10	A2
Loscoe Close	8	A2
Louisa Street	1	C2
Lovaine Grove	25	A1
Love Lane (Castleford)	1	C2
Love Lane (Ossett)	13	A2
Love Lane (Pontefract)	9 C3/19	C1
Love Lane (Wakefield)	15	A1
Love Lane	T/C	B2
Love Lane Terrace	9	C3
Low Cross Court	11	C1
Low Farm Lane	29	A2
Low Fold	13	B2

Street	Page	Grid	Street	Page	Grid	Street	Page	Grid	Street	Page	Grid
Low Gate	41	C2	Manor Road (Horbury)	13	C3	Mayfield Court	13	B3	Mill Lane (Streethouse)	17	C2
Low Green (Ackworth)	29	A2	Manor Road (Ossett)	14	A2	Mayfield Rise	35	B2	Mill Street (Castleford)	1	C2
Low Green (Knottingley)	12	A1	Manor Road (Wakefield)	14	C2	Mayfields Way	40	C3	Mill Street (South Kirkby)	40	B3
Low Lane	22	B1/C2	Manor Road (Walton)	25	C2	Mayor's Walk Avenue	20	A1	Mill View (Hemsworth)	36	C3
Low Moor Crescent	32	C1	Manor View	2	B3	Mayor's Walk Close	20	A1	Mill View (Knottingley)	11	A1
Low Moor Lane	32	B2/C2	Manorcroft	7	B3	Mayor's Walk	20	A1	Millars Walk	40	B2
Lower Cambridge Street	2	A2	Manorfield Drive	13	C3	Mayors Walk	3	B2	Millcroft Close	5	C1
Lower Northcroft	41	B2	Manorfields Avenue	26	C2	Mclaren Avenue	39	A3	Millcroft Rise	5	C1
Lower Northfield Lane	40	C2	Manorfields Court	26	C1	Meadow Bank (Ackworth)	29	A1	Millcroft	5	C1
Lower Oxford Street	2	A2	Manygates Avenue	15	C3	Meadow Bank (Havercroft)	35	C2	Miller Avenue	25	A1
Lower Station Road	7	B3	Manygates Court	15	C3	Meadow Brook Chase	7	C3	Miller Court	33	B1
Lower Taythes Lane	10	C3	Manygates Crescent	15	C3	Meadow Brook Close	7	C3	Miller Garth	29	A3
Lower Warrengate	15	B1	Manygates Lane	15	C3/25 A1	Meadow Brook Court	7	C3	Millfield Cottages	24	A2
Lower Warrengate	T/C	D2	Manygates Park	15	C3	Meadow Brook Green	7	C3	Millfield Crescent	19	C1
Lower York Street	15	B1	Maple Avenue	20	A2	Meadow Close (Hemsworth)	36	C3	Millfield Road	23	C1
Lower York Street	T/C	D1	Maple Close	1	C3	Meadow Close (Outwood)	5	B1	Millfields	13	A2
Lowfield Crescent	37	A3	Maple Drive	20	A2	Meadow Court (Castleford)	3	A2	Millgate	29	A3
Lowfield Road	37	A2	Maple Grove (Normanton)	17	B1	Meadow Court (Netherton)	23	A2	Millstone Close	29	A3
Lowswater Road	11	B3	Maple Grove (Pontefract)	20	A2	Meadow Court (South Elmsall)	41	C2	Millward Street	35	B2
Lumley Avenue	1	B2	Maple Street	14	C1	Meadow Croft (Hemsworth)	37	A3	Milne's Avenue	14	C3
Lumley Hill	1	B2	Maple Walk	11	B2	Meadow Croft (Outwood)	5	B1	Milner Street	13	A1
Lumley Mount	1	B2	Mapplewell Crescent	13	B2	Meadow Garth	5	B1	Milner Way	13	B2
Lumley Street	1	B2	Mapplewell Drive	13	B2	Meadow Lane	14	C1	Milner's Lane	21	A2
Lund Hill Lane	35	A3	March Street	7	A3	Meadow Rise	36	C3	Milnes Grove	2	C2
Lupset Crescent	14	C3	Marchant Street	1	C1	Meadow Road	1	C3	Milnthorpe Crescent	25	A2
Lynda Grove	13	C3	Margaret Street (Outwood)	5	A2	Meadow Vale (Outwood)	5	B1	Milnthorpe Drive	25	A2
Lyndale Drive	4	C3	Margaret Street	15	A1	Meadow Vale (Netherton)	23	A3	Milnthorpe Green	25	A2
Lyndale Grove	7	C3	Margaret Street	T/C	B1	Meadow View	13	A1	Milnthorpe Lane	15 C3/25 A2	
Lynwood Close (Knottingley)	11	C1	Marine Villa Road	11	B1	Meadow Walk	38	A1	Milton Close	24	A2
Lynwood Close (Streethouse)	18	A2	Marion Avenue	4	B3	Meadow Way	29	A1	Milton Court	5	C1
Lynwood Crescent (Fitzwilliam)	36	B1	Marion Close	40	B3	Meadow, The	17	B1	Milton Crescent	14	B2
Lynwood Crescent (Pontefract)	20	A2	Marion Grove	4	B3	Meadowcroft Close	5	C1	Milton Drive	36	C1
Lynwood Drive	25	A2	Marizon Grove	T/C	D1	Meadowcroft Court	5	C1	Milton Place	13	B2
Lyon Road	20	A2	Mark Street	15	B2	Meadowcroft Road	5	C1	Milton Road	14	B3
			Market Place (Normanton)	7	B3	Meadowfield Close	36	B1	Milton Street (Castleford)	1	C1

M

Street	Page	Grid	Street	Page	Grid	Street	Page	Grid	Street	Page	Grid
			Market Place (Ossett)	13	B2	Meadowfield Court	6	B1	Milton Street (Wakefield)	15	A2
			Market Place (Pontefract)	10	A3	Meadowfields Close	26	C1	Milton Street	T/C	A3
Mackie Hill Close	24	A3	Market Place (South Elmsall)	41	B2	Meadowfields Drive	26	C1	Milton Terrace	36	B1
Mackinnon Avenue	7	C2	Market Street (Featherstone)	18	C1	Meadowfields Rise	6	B1	Minden Close	19	C1
Madeley Road	35	C2	Market Street (Hemsworth)	37	A3	Meadowfields Road	26	C2	Minden Way	19	C1
Madeley Square	3	A1	Market Street (Normanton)	7	B3	Meadowgate	13	A1	Minsthorpe Lane	38 B3/41 B1	
Magdalene Road	14	B2	Market Street (Wakefield)	15	B1	Meadway	17	C2	Minsthorpe Vale	41	B2
Magna Grove	25	A1	Market Street	T/C	C2	Medley Street	2	A2	Mirey Butt Lane	11	B2
Main Street (Badsworth)	38	A1	Market Way	T/C	D2	Medlock Road	23	B1	Mitchells Yard	13	B2
Main Street (North Elmsall)	39	A2	Markham Street	15	A2	Melbourne Avenue	4	C2	Molly Hurst Lane	32	C3
Main Street	35	C3	Markham Street	T/C	A3	Melbourne Mews	4	C2	Mona Street	14	C1
Major Street	15	B3	Marl Pit Hill	19	C1	Melbourne Road	5	A3	Monckton Drive	2	C2
Makin Street	T/C	A3	Marlborough Croft	41	B1	Mellwood Lane	41	B2	Monckton Road	15	A3
Malham Road	16	A1	Marlborough Street (Ossett)	13	A2	Melton Close	41	B1	Monk Street	15	C2
Malham Square	16	A1	Marlborough Street (Wakefield)	15	A2	Melton Road	24	B3	Monk Street	T/C	E3
Mallard Avenue	25	A3	Marlborough Street	T/C	B3	Merewood Road	1	A2	Monkhill Avenue	10	B2
Mallard Road	1	C2	Marlpit Lane	21	A2	Methley Road	1	B2	Monkhill Drive	10	A2
Malt Kiln Croft	25	B1	Marriot Grove	25	B1	Mews Court (Featherstone)	19	A2	Monkhill Lane	10	A2
Maltings, The	10	A3	Marsh End	12	A1	Mews Court (Ossett)	13	A2	Monkhill Mount	10	A2
Maltins, The	2	A1	Marsh Lane	12	A1	Mews, The	7	B2	Monkroyd Cottages	19	B1
Maltkiln Drive	31	C2	Marsh Lea Grove	37	B2	Michael Avenue	5	C1	Monkwood Road	5	A2
Maltkiln Lane	2	A1	Marsh Way	15	B1	Micklegate Square	10	A3	Montague Street	15	C3
Malton Road	39	A2	Marsh Way	T/C	C1	Micklegate	10	A3	Montague Street	16	A3
Malvern Close	1	A3	Marshall Avenue	32	C1	Micklethwaite Road	32	C1	Montcalm Crescent	6	A2
Malvern Road	11	B1	Marshall Drive	41	B2	Middle Field Lane	32	C3	Monument Lane	20	B1
Manor Avenue	13	C3	Marshall Hill	16	C1	Middle Lane (Crofton)	27	A2	Monument Mews	20	B1
Manor Close (Badsworth)	38	A1	Marshall Street	6	A1	Middle Lane (Featherstone)	18	C2	Moor Avenue	5	C1
Manor Close (Notton)	34	A3	Marsland Avenue	15	C1	Middle Lane (Knottingley)	11	C2	Moor Bridge	20	B3
Manor Close (Ossett)	13	C3	Marsland Avenue	T/C	E2	Middle Oxford Street	1	C2	Moor Grove	5	C1
Manor Court	13	C3	Marsland Place	T/C	E2	Middleton Way	11	B1	Moor Lane (Pontefract)	20	C2/C3
Manor Crescent (Lupset)	14	C2	Marsland Street	T/C	E2	Midland Road	10	B3	Moor Lane (Upton)	38	B3
Manor Crescent (Walton)	25	C2	Marsland Terrace	15	C1	Mildred Sylvester Way	7 C3/8 A2		Moor Lane (Wentbridge)	30	B1
Manor Croft	35	C3	Marsland Terrace	T/C	E2	Mill Close (Ackworth)	29	A2	Moor Road (Featherstone)	19	A2
Manor Drive (Crofton)	26	C2	Marston Court	1	B3	Mill Close (South Kirkby)	40	B3	Moor Road (Stanley)	5	C1
Manor Drive (Featherstone)	8	C3	Marston Walk	6	C2	Mill Cottages	18	B2	Moor Top Avenue	28	C3
Manor Drive (Ossett)	13	C3	Martin Frobisher Drive	7	A2	Mill Dam Lane	10	B3	Moor Top Drive	37	A3
Manor Farm Court	24	A3	Martin Grove	25	B2	Mill Farm Drive	25	A3	Moor View Close	2	B2
Manor Farm Estate	41	C2	Martin Street	17	B1	Mill Garth	20	A1	Moor View	24	B3
Manor Farm Road	24	A3	Marton Avenue	36	C3	Mill Hill (Ackworth)	29	A1	Moorcroft Street	13	B2
Manor Garth	25	C2	Marton Drive	24	B3	Mill Hill (Normanton)	7	B3	Moorfield Crescent	37	A3
Manor Grove (Glass Houghton)	2	A3	Mary Rose Court	18	C2	Mill Hill Avenue	19	C1	Moorfield Place	36	C3
Manor Grove (Ossett)	13	C3	Marygate	15	B1	Mill Hill Close	21	A2	Moorhouse Avenue (Stanley))	6	B1
Manor Grove (South Kirkby)	40	B3	Marygate	T/C	C2	Mill Hill Lane (Darrington)	21	A1	Moorhouse Avenue (Wakefield)	15	A1
Manor Haigh Road	14	C2/C3	Matty Marsden Lane	13	B3	Mill Hill Lane (Pontefract)	19	C1	Moorhouse Avenue	T/C	A2
Manor House Bungalows	11	C1	Maudeline Bridge	15	A2	Mill Hill Road	20	A1	Moorhouse Close (Normanton)	7	C2
Manor House	34	A2	Maudeline Bridge	T/C	B3	Mill Lane (Ackworth)	29	A3	Moorhouse Close (Stanley)	6	B1
Manor Lane	13	C3	Mauds Yard	10	A3	Mill Lane (Castleford)	2	A1	Moorhouse Court Mews	41	C3
Manor Park Avenue	10	B2	Maxwell Street	18	C2	Mill Lane (Normanton)	7	C1	Moorhouse Court	41	C3
Manor Park Rise	21	B2	May Bush Road	15	C3	Mill Lane (Pontefract)	10	B2	Moorhouse Crescent	15	A1
Manor Park	21	A2	Maybury Avenue	24	B2	Mill Lane (Ryhill)	35	B2	Moorhouse Grove	6	B1
Manor Place	23	B1	Mayfair Place	37	A2	Mill Lane (South Elmsall)	41	C1	Moorhouse Lane	27	A3
Manor Rise	25	C2	Mayfair	10	A2	Mill Lane (South Kirkby)	40	B3	Moorhouse Terrace	6	B1

Street	Page	Grid
Moorhouse View (South Elmsall)	41	C3
Moorhouse View (Stanley)	6	B1
Moorland Drive	32	C1
Moorlands Avenue	13	A1
Moorroyd Street	13	A1
Moorshutt Road	36	C3
Moorside Crescent	32	C1
Morley Avenue	11	C2
Morrell Crescent	4	C2
Morris Close	36	B1
Morrison Street	2	A2
Mortimer Close	13	C2
Mortimer Row	23	B1
Morton Crescent	2	B2
Morton Parade	15	A2
Morton Parade	T/C	A3
Morvern Meadows	37	B3
Moss Street	1	C1
Mostyn Walk	32	C1
Mount Avenue (Hemsworth)	36	C2
Mount Avenue (Wrenthorpe)	4	C2
Mount Crescent	14	C3
Mount Pleasant (Ackworth)	29	A2
Mount Pleasant (Castleford)	2	B2
Mount Pleasant (Walton)	16	A3
Mount Pleasant Street	19	A1
Mount Road	6	A1
Mount Walk	2	A3
Mount, The (Castleford)	2	C2
Mount, The (Normanton)	7	B3
Mount, The (Pontefract)	10	A3
Mount, The (Wakefield)	14	C3
Mount, The (Wrenthorpe)	4	B3
Mountbatten Avenue (Outwood)	5	B2
Mountbatten Avenue (Sandal)	25	B1
Mountbatten Crescent	5	B2
Mountbatten Grove	5	B2
Mountfields Walk	40	C3
Mourning Field Lane	39	A1
Moverley Flatts	20	B1
Moxon Close	20	A1
Moxon Grove	5	A2
Moxon Place	14	B2
Moxon Square	15	C1
Moxon Square	T/C	E1
Moxon Street	5	B2
Moxon Way	5	B2
Muirfield Avenue	9	A3
Muirfield Drive	15	A3
Mulberry Avenue	35	B2
Mulberry Place	35	B2
Myson Avenue	10	B2

N

Street	Page	Grid
Navigation Road	2	A1
Navigation Yard	15	C2
Navigation Yard	T/C	C2
Navvy Lane	34	C2
Naylor Street	13	A1
Nell Gap Avenue	22	B2
Nell Gap Crescent	22	B2
Nell Gap Lane	22	B2
Nelson Street (Normanton)	7	C2
Nelson Street (South Hiendley)	36	A3
Nestfield Close	10	A2
Neston Way	13	B1
Netherfield Avenue	22	C3
Netherfield Close	1	B3
Netherfield Crescent	22	C3
Netherfield Place	22	C3
Netherly Brow	13	B3
Netheroyd Court	17	B3
Netheroyd Place	17	B3
Netheroyd	17	C2
Netherton Hall Gardens	23	A2
Netherton Lane	23	A1/A2
Nettle Lane	15	B1
Nettle Lane	T/C	E2
Nettleton Buildings	13	B1
Nettleton Chase	13	A1
Nettleton Street (Ossett)	13	A2
Nettleton Street (Stanley)	6	B1
Neville Close	40	C2
Neville Road	14	B2
Neville Street (Normanton)	7	B3
Neville Street (Wakefield)	15	C3
Nevison Avenue	10	B2
New Brunswick Street	15	B2
New Hall Close	24	A3
New Hall Lane	22	A3
New Hall Approach	22	A3
New Lane (Durkar)	24	B2
New Lane (Normanton)	7	C2
New Lane (Pontefract)	10	A3
New Lane (Upton)	38	B3
New Lane Crescent	38	B3
New Park Lane	14	A1
New Road (Badsworth)	38	A1
New Road (Horbury)	23	C1
New Road (Middlestown)	22	B2
New Road (Snydale)	17	C1
New Road (West Hardwick)	28	A1
New Road (Woolley)	33	A3
New Row (Badsworth)	38	A1
New Row (Kirkhamgate)	4	A3
New Row Cottages	21	A3
New Street (Ackworth)	28	C3
New Street (Castleford)	2	A1
New Street (Horbury)	23	C1
New Street (Kinsley)	36	C1
New Street (Moorthorpe)	41	A2
New Street (Ossett)	13	B2
New Street (South Hiendley)	35	C3
New Wellgate	2	B2
New Wells	15	B2
New Wells	T/C	D3
Newall Crescent	36	B1
Newbury Drive	41	B1
Newfield Avenue (Castleford)	2	A2
Newfield Avenue (Normanton)	7	C3
Newfield Close	7	C3
Newfield Court	7	C3
Newfield Crescent	7	C3
Newgate	10	A3
Newhill	40	C3
Newlaithes Crescent	7	C3
Newland Court	15	C3
Newland Crescent	24	B2
Newland Lane	6	C3/7 A3
Newland Street (Knottingley)	11	A1
Newland Street (Wakefield)	15	C3
Newland View	7	A2
Newlands Drive	5	C1
Newlands Walk	5	C1
Newlyn Drive	25	A1
Newport Street	9	C3
Newsholme Lane	24	B2
Newstead Avenue (Fitzwilliam)	36	B1
Newstead Avenue (Outwood)	5	A2
Newstead Crescent	36	B1
Newstead Drive	36	B1
Newstead Grove	36	B1
Newstead Lane	36	A1
Newstead Road	15	A1
Newstead Road	T/C	B1
Newstead Terrace	36	B1
Newstead View	36	B1
Newton Avenue	5	B3
Newton Close	5	B3
Newton Court	5	B2
Newton Drive (Castleford)	2	C2
Newton Drive (Outwood)	5	B2
Newton Green	5	B3
Newton Lane	5	B2
Newtons Building	4	B2
Nicholson Street	1	C2
Nidd Drive	2	C1
Nightingale Crest	14	B2
Ninevah Lane	38	A1
Nooking, The	4	A2
Noon Close	5	C1
Norman House	7	B3
Normans Way	25	B1
Normanton Street	23	C1
Normanton View	7	B3
North Avenue (Castleford)	1	B2
North Avenue (Horbury)	23	C1
North Avenue (Pontefract)	19	C1
North Avenue (South Elmsall)	41	B2
North Avenue (Wakefield)	5	B3
North Bailey Gate	10	B3
North Close	8	C3
North Cottages	23	B1
North Crescent	41	C1
North Drive	25	A3
North Ives	10	A3
North Lodge Lane	21	C2
North Road Terrace	15	B1
North Road Terrace	T/C	C1
North Street (Castleford)	1	C2
North Street (Normanton)	17	A1
North Street (South Kirkby)	40	C2
North View (Fitzwilliam)	36	B1
North View (Knottingley)	11	B1
North Walk	37	A3
Northcote	13	A1
Northcroft Avenue	41	C2
Northcroft	41	B2
Northfield Avenue (Knottingley)	11	C2
Northfield Avenue (Ossett)	13	B2
Northfield Avenue (South Kirkby)	40	C2
Northfield Drive	10	B3
Northfield Grove	40	C2
Northfield Lane (Horbury)	23	C1/C2
Northfield Lane (South Kirkby)	40	C2
Northfield Lane (Wakefield)	14	B3
Northfield Road (Knottingley)	11	C2
Northfield Road (Ossett)	13	B2
Northfield Road (Sharlston)	17	B3
Northfield Street	40	C2
Northfield Terrace	14	B3
Northgate (Horbury)	23	B1
Northgate (Pontefract)	10	A3
Northgate (South Hiendley)	36	A3
Northgate (Wakefield)	15	B1
Northgate	T/C	C1
Northgate Close	10	A3
Northland Cottages	10	A3
Northland View	10	A3
Norton Road	15	C1
Norton Road	T/C	E1
Norton Street	15	C2
Norwood Road	37	A3
Norwood Street	7	C2
Norwood	20	C2
Nostell Lane	35	B1
Notton Lane	34	B3
Nunn's Avenue	19	A3
Nunn's Close	19	A3
Nunn's Court	18	C3
Nunn's Croft	19	A2
Nunn's Green	19	A3
Nunn's Lane	19	A2
Nunn's View	18	C3

O

Street	Page	Grid
Oak Avenue	6	A2
Oak Street (Crofton)	26	C2
Oak Street (Outwood)	5	B2
Oak Street (South Elmsall)	41	B3
Oak Tree Grove	37	B3
Oak Tree Meadow	25	C2
Oak Way	7	B3
Oakdale Close	5	A1
Oakenshaw Lane	16 A3/25	C2
Oakenshaw Street	15	C3
Oakes Street	14	B1
Oakfield Crescent	11	B2
Oakfield Park	30	B3
Oakland Drive	22	C3
Oakland Road (Netherton)	22	C3
Oakland Road	15	C3
Oaklands Croft	25	C2
Oakleigh Avenue	14	B2
Oaktree Lane	29	B3
Oakwell Avenue	19	C1
Oakwell Close	36	B1
Oakwood Avenue	14	B2
Oakwood Close	7	A2
Oakwood Cottages	13	B2
Oakwood Drive (Altofts)	7	A2
Oakwood Drive (Hemsworth)	37	A3
Oakwood Gardens	24	A2
Oakwood Grove	23	C1
Oakwood	14	B3
Offley Lane	28	A3
Old Church Street	13	B2
Old Crown Road	14	B3
Old Great North Road (Darrington)	21	B3
Old Great North Road (Ferrybridge)	11	A1
Old Lane	31	A2
Old Mill Close	36	C3
Old Mill Road	13	A3
Old Mill Yard	13	A3
Old Mount Farm	33	A3
Old Orchard, The	37	A2
Old Potovens Lane	5	A2
Old Road (Knottingley)	11	A1
Old Road (Middlestown)	22	A3
Olive Villas	19	C1
Olivers Mount	10	B3
Orchard Avenue	5	C1
Orchard Avenue	6	A1
Orchard Close (Outwood)	4	C2
Orchard Croft (Horbury)	23	C1
Orchard Croft (Walton)	25	C2
Orchard Croft (Wrenthorpe)	4	C2
Orchard Drive (Ackworth)	29	A3
Orchard Drive (Durkar)	24	B2
Orchard Drive (South Hiendley)	35	C3
Orchard Gardens	24	B2
Orchard Head Crescent	10	B2
Orchard Head Drive (South Hiendley)	10	B2
Orchard Head Lane	10	A2
Orchard Road	25	B1
Orchard View (Ackworth)	29	A3
Orchard View (Darrington)	21	A2
Orchard, The (Crofton)	26	C1
Orchard, The (Featherstone)	9	A3
Orchard, The (Ossett)	13	B2
Orchard, The (Pontefract)	20	B2
Orchard, The (Wrenthorpe)	4	C2
Orwell Close	3	A3
Osborne Avenue	14	B3
Otters Holt	24	B2
Ouchthorpe Fold	5	B2
Ouchthorpe Lane	5	B2
Outwood Park Court	5	A2
Oval, The	34	B3
Owl Lane	13	A1
Owler's Lane	30 A3/38	B1
Oxford Court Gardens	1	C2
Oxford Road	5	A3
Oxford Street (Featherstone)	19	A2
Oxford Street (Normanton)	7	C2
Oxford Street (South Elmsall)	41	B3
Oxford Street (Wakefield)	15	C3

P

Street	Page	Grid
Pacaholme Road	4	B3
Paddock View	2	C2
Paddock, The (Normanton)	7	B3
Paddock, The (Townville)	2	C2
Paddock, The (Woolley)	33	A3
Painthorpe Lane	24 A3/32	C1
Painthorpe Terrace	24	A3
Paleside Lane	13	B1
Palesides Avenue	13	B1
Palmer's Avenue	41	C2
Pannal Avenue	5	C3
Paradise Fields	10	A3
Park Lodge Court	15	C1
Park Avenue (Castleford)	2	B2
Park Avenue (Darrington)	21	A2
Park Avenue (Kirkthorpe)	16	C1
Park Avenue (Normanton)	7	B2
Park Avenue (Outwood)	5	A2/B1
Park Avenue (Pontefract)	9	C3
Park Avenue (South Kirkby)	40	C2
Park Avenue (Wakefield)	15	B2
Park Close	21	A2
Park Court	13	C3
Park Crescent	2 C2/3	A2
Park Crest	36	C3
Park Drive	5	B1
Park Estate	40	C2
Park Gardens	13	C3
Park Green	7	A3
Park Grove Road	15	A2
Park Grove Road	T/C	A3

Street	Map	Grid
Park Grove	13	C3
Park Hill Crescent	15	C1
Park Hill Grove	15	C1
Park Hill Lane	15	C1
Park Hill Lane	T/C	F2
Park Lane (Bretton)	31	C3
Park Lane (Pontefract)	9	B3
Park Lodge Crescent	15	C1
Park Lodge Crescent	T/C	F2
Park Lodge Grove	15	C1
Park Lodge Grove	T/C	E2
Park Lodge Lane	15 C1/16	A1
Park Lodge Lane	T/C	F2
Park Mill Lane	4 A3/13	C1
Park Place	9	C3
Park Rise	2	B2
Park Road	2	B3
Park Square (Ossett)	13	C3
Park Square (Outwood)	5	B1
Park Street (Horbury)	23	B1
Park Street (Ossett)	13	C3
Park Street (Wakefield)	15	B2
Park Street	T/C	E3
Park Terrace	41	C2
Park View (Kinsley)	36	C2
Park View (Lofthouse Gate)	5	B1
Park View (Townville)	2	C3
Park View	14	C1
Park Villas Drive	9	C3
Parker Avenue	7	A2
Parker Road	23	C1
Parkfield Drive	14	A2
Parkfield Lane	8	C3
Parkfield View	14	A2
Parkgate Avenue	15	C1
Parkgate Avenue	T/C	F2
Parkgate	40	C3
Parkinson Close	15	C1
Parklands (Castleford)	2	A2
Parklands (Ossett)	13	C3
Parklands Avenue	23	A1
Parklands Court	23	A1
Parklands Crescent	23	A1
Parklands Drive	23	A1
Parkside Lane	5	C3
Parkside	3	A1
Parkway	26	B1
Parliament Square	T/C	B2
Parliament Street	15	A1
Parson Lane	33	A2
Partons Place	5	B1
Paterson Avenue	15	A2
Paterson Avenue	T/C	A2
Patience Lane	7	A2
Patterson Court	4	C2
Pauline Terrace	1	C2
Peach Tree Close	19	C1
Peacock Avenue	14	C1
Peacock Close	14	C1
Peacock Grove	14	C1
Pear Tree Close	19	C1
Pear Tree Lane	37	A2
Pear Tree Walk	15	A1
Pearson Street	7	B1
Peartree Field Lane	30	C3
Pease Close	20	A1
Peel Close	23	C1
Peel Street	23	C1
Pemberton Road	2	C1
Penarth Avenue	38	B3
Penarth Terrace	38	B3
Pendennis Avenue	41	A1
Penlington Close	37	A3
Pennine Close	14	B3
Pennine View	38	B2
Pennine Way	37	B3
Penrith Crescent	3	A1
Penrose Place	24	B3
Penrose Beck Drive	28	C3
Pentland Avenue	11	B2
Pentland Grove	14	C1
Percy Street	40	C2
Perseverance Street	1	C1
Peterson Road	15	C1
Peterson Road	T/C	E2
Philip Garth	5	B1
Philip's Lane	21	A2
Philips Grove	5	B1
Phillips Street	1	C1
Phoenix Court	15	A1
Phoenix Court	T/C	A2
Phoenix Street	41	B2
Piccadilly	15	A2
Piccadilly	T/C	B2
Pickering Drive	13	A1
Pickering Lane	13	A1
Pickersgill Street	13	A1
Pildacre Brow	13	A2
Pildacre Crescent	13	A2
Pildacre Lane	13	A2
Pilkington Street	15	B3
Pinder's Grove	5	C3
Pinderfields Road	15	B1
Pinderfields Road	T/C	D1
Pinders Crescent	11	A1
Pinders Garth	11	A1
Pine Close	2	A2
Pine Street	41	B3
Pine Tree Avenue	19	C2
Pinewood Avenue	14	B2
Pinewood Place	11	B2
Pinfold Close	11	A1
Pinfold Drive	26	C1
Pinfold Grove	25	A1
Pinfold Lane	25	B1
Pippin's Approach	7	B2
Pippins Green Avenue	4	A2
Plane Green	10	B3
Pledwick Crescent	25	A3
Pledwick Drive	25	A3
Pledwick Grove	25	A3
Pledwick Lane	25	A3
Pledwick Rise	25	A3
Plimsoll Street	37	A3
Plum Tree Close	19	C1
Plumpton Place	15	A2
Plumpton Place	T/C	A3
Plumpton Road	15	A2
Plumpton Road	T/C	A3
Plumpton Street	T/C	A3
Plumpton Terrace	15	A2
Plumpton Terrace	T/C	A3
Pollard Street	5	B1
Pollard's Fields	3	C3
Polperro Close	7	B2
Pomfret Court	20	C1
Pontefract Lane	38	B2
Pontefract Road (Ackworth)	29 A1/37	B1
Pontefract Road (Castleford)	2	A2
Pontefract Road (Crofton)	17	A3
Pontefract Road (Featherstone)	19 B2/C3	
Pontefract Road (Ferrybridge)	10	B2
Pontefract Road (Knottingley)	11	A2
Pontefract Road (Normanton)	7	C2
Pontefract Terrace	37	A3
Pope Street	7	C1
Poplar Avenue (Castleford)	3	A2
Poplar Avenue (Wakefield)	14	B2
Poplar Drive	7	A1
Poplar Green	10	B3
Poplar Grove (Knottingley)	11	B2
Poplar Grove (Pontefract)	19	C1
Poplar Street	5	B1
Poplar Terrace	41	B2
Poplar View	10	A3
Poplars, The	12	A2
Portland Avenue	9	C3
Portland Croft	9	C3
Portland Place	38	B3
Portland Street	16	A3
Portobello Grove	15	B3
Portobello Road	15	B3
Post Office Road	19	A2
Pothill Lane	38	C2
Potovens Lane	4	C2
Potter Avenue	14	C2
Potters Croft	5	B1
Pottery Lane	11	B1
Pottery Street	1	C1
Potts' Terrace	7	B3
Powell Street (Castleford)	2	A2
Powell Street (South Kirkby)	41	A2
Poxton Grove	41	A3
Prail Close	10	B3
Prail Lane	10	B3
Prestwick Fold	13	B1
Pretoria Street (Castleford)	2	C2
Pretoria Street (Featherstone)	18	C1
Pretoria Street (Wakefield)	15	C3
Primrose Close	20	A1
Primrose Drive	2	C2
Primrose Hill	11	C1
Primrose Lane	24	A2
Primrose Vale	11	C1
Prince William Court	18	C2
Princess Avenue	41	B2
Princess Street (Castleford)	2	A1
Princess Street (Normanton)	7	B3
Princess Street (Outwood)	5	A2
Princess Street (Wakefield)	15	C3
Priordale Road	18	C2
Priory Close (Altofts)	7	A2
Priory Close (Ossett)	13	B2
Priory Croft	13	B2
Priory Estate	41	C2
Priory Grange	10	B2
Priory Mews	5	C1
Priory Road (Featherstone)	18	C2
Priory Road (Ossett)	13	B2
Priory Square	25	C2
Prospect Avenue	7	B2
Prospect Lane	23	C1
Prospect Road	13	B2
Prospect Street	23	C1
Prospect Terrace (Knottingley)	11	C1
Prospect Terrace (South Kirkby)	40	C2
Providence Street	15	B1
Providence Street	T/C	C1
Pugneys Road	15	B3
Pump Lane	28	A1
Purston Lane	28	C1
Purston Park Court	19	A2

Q

Street	Map	Grid
Quaker House Yard	15	C2
Quarry Avenue	11	C2
Quarry Buildings	23	B1
Quarry Hill	23	B1
Quarry Lane	38	B2
Quarry Mount	35	B2
Quarry Street	29	A3
Quarry View	28	C3
Quarrydene Drive	2	C2
Quebec Street	15	A2
Quebec Street	T/C	B3
Queen Elizabeth Drive	17	B1
Queen Elizabeth Grove	15	C1
Queen Elizabeth Grove	T/C	F1
Queen Elizabeth House	15	C1
Queen Elizabeth House	T/C	F1
Queen Elizabeth Road	15	C1
Queen Elizabeth Road	T/C	F1
Queen Elizabeth Street	5	A2
Queen Street (Castleford)	2	A1
Queen Street (Horbury)	23	B1
Queen Street (Normanton)	7	B3
Queen Street (Outwood)	5	A2
Queen Street (Pontefract)	9	C3
Queen Street (Wakefield)	15	B1
Queen Street	T/C	C2
Queen Street (South Elmsall)	41	B2
Queen's Avenue	19	C1
Queen's Crescent (Ossett)	13	B2
Queen's Crescent (Sharlston)	17	B3
Queen's Gardens	13	B2
Queen's Park Drive	2	B2
Queen's Road	19	C1
Queen's Square	19	C1
Queen's Street	13	B2
Queen's Terrace (Ossett)	13	B2
Queen's Terrace (Pontefract)	9	C3
Queen's Walk	13	C2
Queens Drive (Osset)	13	C2
Queens Drive (Wrenthorpe)	4	C3
Queens Drive Close	13	C2
Queens Park Close	2	C2
Queens Road	2	C2
Queens Terrace	23	B1
Queensbury Avenue	5	B1
Queensway (Normanton)	17	B1
Queensway (Pontefract)	10	B2

R

Street	Map	Grid
Racca Avenue	12	A1
Racca Green	11	C1
Rachael Street	23	B1
Radcliffe Place	T/C	C2
Radcliffe Road	14	B2
Radford Park Avenue	40	C2
Rae Court	5	C1
Raglan Close	1	B1
Railway Avenue	10	A3
Railway Cottages (Ackworth)	29	A3
Railway Cottages (North Elmsall)	39	A3
Railway Terrace (Featherstone)	19	A2
Railway Terrace (Fitzwilliam)	36	B1
Railway Terrace (Normanton)	7	A3
Railway Terrace (Outwood)	5	A1
Railway View (Castleford)	1	C2
Railway View (Stanley)	5	C1
Rainsborough Avenue	11	A2
Ramsden Street	1	C3
Ramsey Crescent	22	B2
Ramsey Road	22	B2
Ramsey View	22	B2
Ranter's Fold	23	B1
Ravel Lane	35	B3
Ravensknowle Cottages	19	B2
Ravensmead	19	B2
Rawgate Avenue	1	B2
Rayner Street	23	B1
Rectory Avenue	1	C1
Rectory Garth	37	A2
Rectory Street	1	C1
Red Hall Lane	5	A3
Red Lane	17 A2/18	A2
Redhill Avenue	2	B2
Redhill Drive	2	C2
Redhill Gardens	2	C2
Redhill Mount	2	B2
Redhill Road	2	B2
Redhill View	2	B2
Redland Crescent	36	C1
Redmayne Grove	11	B2
Redruth Drive	7	B2
Regent Crescent	36	A3
Regent Street (Castleford)	1	C2
Regent Street (Featherstone)	18	C2
Regent Street (Hemsworth)	36	C2
Regent Street (Horbury)	23	B1
Regent Street (Normanton)	7	C2
Regent Street (South Elmsall)	41	A2
Regent Street (South Hiendley)	36	A3
Regent Street (Wakefield)	15	C3
Regents Park	15	C1
Regents Park	T/C	F2
Regina Crescent	35	C2
Reid Park Avenue	23	A1
Renfield Grove	7	C2
Rhodes Crescent	20	A1
Rhodes Gardens	5	B1
Rhodes Street	1	C1
Rhyddings Avenue	28	C3
Rhyddings Drive	28	C3
Rhyl Street	19	A1
Richard Street	T/C	D1
Richmond Avenue	3 C3/11	A1
Richmond Court (Pontefract)	10	A3
Richmond Court (Crofton)	26	C1
Richmond Garth	13	C3
Richmond Road (Upton)	38	B3
Richmond Road (Wakefield)	5	B3
Richmond Street	2	A2
Richmond Terrace	10	A3
Richworth Street	T/C	C1
Riddings Close	37	A3
Ridge Avenue	22	B2
Ridge Crescent	22	B2
Ridge Road	22	B2
Ridgedale Mount	3	A3
Ridgefield Street	1	C2
Ridgestone Avenue	37	A3
Ridgeway Square	11	C2

Name	Page	Grid	Name	Page	Grid	Name	Page	Grid	Name	Page	Grid	Name	Page	Grid
Ridgeway, The	11	C2	Royd Head Farm	13	A2	St John's Mews	15	A1	School Close	17	B2
Ridings Close	5	B1	Royd Moor Lane	37	C2	St John's Mount	15	A1	School Crescent	14	B3
Ridings Court	5	B1	Royds Avenue (Castleford)	2	C1	St John's North	15	A1	School Drive	11	A1
Ridings Gardens	5	A1	Royds Avenue (Gawthorpe)	13	A1	St John's Square	15	A1	School Hill	24	C3
Ridings Lane	5	B1	Royds Grove	5	B1	St John's Square	T/C		School Lane (Glass Houghton)	2	B2
Ridings Mews	5	A1	Royles Close	40	C3	St John's Street	23	A1	School Lane (Horbury)	23	B1
Ridings Way	5	A1	Rufford Street	14	C1	St Joseph's Mount	19	C1	School Lane (Ryhill)	35	B2
Rigg Lane	29	B2/C2	Runtlings Lane	13	A2	St Leonards Yard	23	B1	School Lane (Walton)	25	C2
Rigley Lane	28	A1	Runtlings Terrace	13	A2	St Luke's Close	22	B2	School Lane (Wrenthorpe)	4	C3
Rill Court	36	C3	Runtlings, The	13	A2	St Lukes Lane	22	B2	School Road (Lupset)	14	B3
Ring O'Bells Yard	23	B1	Rushworth Close	5	C1	St Mark's Street	15	B1	School Road (Willow Park)	20	B1
Ringwood Court	5	B2	Ruskin Avenue	5	A2	St Martin's Grove	1	B2/B3	School Street (Castleford)	2	A1
Ringwood Way	37	B3	Ruskin Close	2	C1	St Martins Close	18	C2	School Street (Gawthorpe)	13	A1
Ripley Close	7	C3	Ruskin Court	4	C3	St Mary's Close	41	C2	School Street (North Elmsall)	39	A2
Ripley Court	7	B3	Ruskin Drive	2	C2	St Mary's Road	7	A2	School Street (Whitwood Mere)	1	C1
Ripley Drive	7	C2	Russell Avenue	32	C1	St Marys Avenue	7	A2	School Yard	23	B1
Rise, The	20	B1	Russell Street	15	B2	St Marys Place	1	C1	Schoolaboards Lane	10	B3
Rishworth Close	4	C3	Russets, The	25	B2	St Michael's Close (Castleford)	2	A2	Seckar Lane	33	A2
Rishworth Street	15	B1	Rustic Cottages	13	B1	St Michael's Close (Wakefield)	15	A2	Secker Street	15	B3
Rivelin Road	1	C2	Rutland Avenue (Pontefract)	20	A2	St Michael's Close	T/C		Second Avenue (Fitzwilliam)	28	A3
River Mead	15	B3	Rutland Avenue (Sandal)	25	A1	St Michaels Avenue	9	C3	Second Avenue (Horbury)	23	A1
River View	1	C1	Rutland Avenue (Wakefield)	15	B3	St Nicholas Street	2	A2	Second Avenue (Outwood)	5	B2
Riverdale Avenue	6	A3	Rutland Drive	16	B3	St Oswald Avenue	19	C1	Second Avenue (South Kirkby)	40	A3
Riverdale Close	6	A3	Ryburn Place	15	B2	St Oswald Road	14	B2	Second Avenue (Upton)	38	B3
Riverdale Crescent	6	A3	Rydal Crescent	14	C1	St Oswald Street	2	A1	Seemore Arcade	13	B2
Riverdale Drive	6	A3	Rydal Drive	14	C1	St Oswalds Place	13	C2	Selby Street	15	B1
Riverdale Road	6	A3	Rydal Street	3	A2	St Paul's Close	38	C2	Selby Street	T/C	D1
Riverside Villas	15	B3	Rydale Mews	13	B3	St Paul's Drive	4	B3	Sessions House Yard	10	A3
Robbins Terrace	19	A1	Ryder Close	9	C3	St Paul's Walk	4	B3	Sewerbridge Lane	8 B3/18 B1
Roberts Way	25	B1	Rye Way	2	C1	St Peter's Crescent	6	B1	Seymour Street	15	B2
Robin Close	10	A2	Ryebread	2	A1	St Peter's Grove	23	C1	Shakespeare Avenue	17	A1
Robin Hood Crescent	14	B3	Ryecroft Avenue	35	C1	St Peters Gate	13	B1	Sharneley Court	20	C1
Robin Hood Street	2	A2	Ryecroft Close	5	B1	St Swithins Court	6	A2	Sharon Cottages	13	B2
Robin Lane	36	B3	Ryecroft Street	13	A2	St Swithins Drive	6	A2	Shaw Close	41	B1
Robinia Walk	15	A1	Ryedale Avenue	11	B2	St Swithins Grove	6	A2	Shaw Fold	25	B1
Robinson Street	10	A3	Ryedale Close	7	B2	St Thomas Road	19	A2	Shay Court	26	B1
Robson Close	20	A1	Ryedale Place	7	B2	St Thomas Terrace	10	B2	Shay Lane (Crofton)	26	B1
Robson's Road	T/C	C2	Ryhill Pits Lane	34	C2/35 A2	Salisbury Close	7	B2	Shay Lane (Walton)	25	C2
Rochester Court	14	B3	Rylstone Grove	5	C3	Salt Pie Alley	15	A2	Sheepwalk Lane (North Elmsall)	39	B2
Rochester Drive	14	B3				Salt Pie Alley	T/C	B3	Sheepwalk Lane (Townville)	3 A2/B3
Rock Hill	2	B2/B3	**S**			Salter Row	10	A3	Sheldrake Road	1	C2
Rock Terrace	2	B2				Saltersgate Avenue	11	B1	Shelley Court	14	B3
Rockingham Lane	29	C3	Saddlers Croft	2	C2	Samuel Drive	5	C1	Shelley Drive	11	A1
Rockingham Street	36	B1	Sagar Street	2	A1	Sand Lane	38	B3	Shelley Walk	5	C1
Rockley Drive	24	C3	St Aiden's Walk	13	C2	Sandal Avenue	25	B1	Shepherd's Hill Bridge	29	A3
Rockwood Crescent	24	A2	St Andrew's Road	3	A1	Sandal Cliff	25	B1	Shepley Street	15	C1
Rodger Lane	4	C3	St Andrews Drive (Featherstone)	9	A3	Sandal Grange Gardens	25	B1	Shepley Street	T/C	F2
Rodney Yard	15	B1	St Andrews Drive (Knottingley)	11	A1	Sandal Hall Mews	25	B1	Shepstye Road	23	B1
Rodney Yard	T/C	C2	St Anne's Street	35	B2	Sandal Rise	30	B3	Sheridan Street	5	B1
Roger Drive	25	A1	St Annes Villas	10	B2	Sanderson Avenue	7	B3	Sherwood Drive	24	B3
Rogers Court	5 C1/6 A1		St Bartholomews Court	14	B2	Sanderson Street	15	C2	Sherwood Grove	14	B2
Roman Rise	20	A2	St Bernard's Avenue	19	C1	Sanderson Street	T/C	E3	Shilling Street	15	B1
Roman Road	30 A1/39 B1		St Botolph's Close	11	C1	Sandford Road	41	B1	Shillinghill Lane	11	A2
Rook's Nest Road	5	C2	St Catherine's Street	15	C3	Sandhill Close	10	A2	Shinwell Drive	39	A2
Rookhill Drive	20	B1	St Clair Street	15	B1	Sandhill Lawn	20	A1	Ship Yard	T/C	E3
Rookhill Mount	20	B1	St Clair Street	T/C	E2	Sandhill Rise	10	A2	Shires Grove	6	A1
Rookhill Road	20	B1	St Clements Court	28	C3	Sandholme Drive	13	B2	Shires Yard	23	B1
Rope Walk	11	C1	St Cuthbert's Court	29	A1	Sandown Avenue	26	C1	Shoe Market	10	A3
Ropergate	10	A3	St Edmunds Close	2	C2	Sandringham Avenue	11	A1	Short Street	18	C2
Rose Avenue	38	B3	St George's Road	14	B3	Sandringham Close	19	C2	Shutt, The	23	C1
Rose Close	38	B3	St Georges Court	35	C1	Sandrock Road	10	B2	Sides Close	20	A1
Rose Farm Close	7	A1	St Georges Walk	25	A2	Sandy Gate Lane	19 C3/29 C1		Sides Road	20	A1
Rose Farm Fold	7	A1	St Giles Avenue	19	C1	Sandy Lane	22	C2	Sike Lane (Walton)	25	C3
Rose Farm Rise	7	A2	St Giles Mount	9 C3/19 C1		Sandy Walk	15	A1	Silcoates Avenue	4	B3
Rose Farm Approach	7	A2	St Helen's Avenue	36	C2	Sandy Walk	T/C	B1	Silcoates Court	4	B3
Rose Garth	26	C1	St Helen's Grove	25	B1	Sandygate Lane	36	C2	Silcoates Drive	4	B3
Rose Grove	38	B3	St Helen's Place	2	A2	Sanquah Terrace	7	C2	Silcoates Lane	4	B3
Rose Lane	28 B3/37 A1		St Ives Close	10	A2	Santingley Lane	26	C2	Silcoates Street	15	A1
Rosedale Avenue	25	B1	St Ives Crescent	3	A3	Saunters Way	7	B2	Silcoates Street	T/C	A1
Rosedale Close	38	C3	St James Court	35	C2	Savile Drive	13	C3	Silkstone Court	7	B2
Rosehill Avenue	36	C3	St James Rise	14	A2	Savile Road	1	C1	Silkstone Crescent	24	C3
Rossiter Drive	11	A2	St James Way	24	B3	Saville Street (Ossett)	13	C3	Silkstone Crest (Altofts)	7	A2
Rosslyn Avenue	28	C3	St James' Park	15	C1	Saville Street Wakefield)	15	B1	Silver Street (Outwood)	5	B2
Rosslyn Court	28	C3	St James' Park	T/C	F2	Saville Street	T/C	C1	Silver Street (Wakefield)	T/C	C2
Rosslyn Grove	28	C3	St John's Avenue (Ossett)	13	C2	Sawley Close	5	C3	Simpson Road	41	C1
Round Street	15	C3	St John's Avenue (Wakefield)	15	A1	Sawwood Close	28	C3	Simpsons Lane	11	B2
Roundhill Road	2	A2	St John's Chase	15	A1	Saxon Avenue	40	B3	Sinclair Garth	25	B2
Roundwood Crescent	14	A2	St John's Close	13	C2	Saxon Close	39	A3	Siward Street	28	A3
Roundwood Rise	14	B2	St John's Court	15	A1	Saxon Grove	40	B3	Skelbrooke Drive	20	A2
Roundwood Road	14	A2	St John's Court	T/C	B1	Saxon Mount	40	B3	Skinner Lane	10	A3
Rowan Avenue	17	B1	St John's Crescent (Normanton)	17	A1	Saxon Way	2	B1	Slack Lane (Crofton)	26	C1
Rowan Court	15	A1	St John's Crescent (Ossett)	13	C2	Saxondale Court	23	B1	Slack Lane (Newmillerdam)	24	C3
Rowan Green	10	B3	St John's Croft	15	A1	Scarth Terrace	6	B1	Slack Lane (South Hiendley)	35	B3
Rowe Close	41	B1	St John's Croft	T/C	B1	Scawthorpe Close	10	B3	Sleep Hill Lane	39	B3
Rowlands Avenue	38	B3	St John's Grove	5	B3	Scholes Road	3	A1	Slutwell Lane	10	A3
Rowley Lane	41	B3				Scholesfield Lane	30	B3	Smallpage Yard	T/C	D2
Royal Court	19	C2				Scholey's Bridge	37	B1	Smawell Lane	34	A2

Street	Page	Grid
Smawthorne Avenue	2	A2
Smawthorne Grove	2	A2
Smawthorne Lane	2	A2
Smeaton Road	39	A3
Smirthwaite Street	15	B1
Smirthwaite View	7	A3
Smith Street	2	B1
Smith Walk	41	B1
Smith Way	13	B2
Smithson Avenue	2	C2
Smithy Close	26	C1
Smithy Lane	22	A3
Smyth Street	15	B1
Smyth Street	T/C	C2
Snapethorpe Crescent	14	B3
Snapethorpe Gate	14	B2
Snapethorpe Road	14	B3
Snowdon Avenue	11	A1
Snowhill Close	5	A3
Snowhill Rise	5	A3
Snydale Avenue	7	C3
Snydale Close	7	C3
Snydale Court	7	C3
Snydale Grove	7	C3
Snydale Road	7	B3
Soho Grove	15	A1
Soho Grove	T/C	A2
Somerset Court	11	C2
Sorrel Close	20	A1
Sotheron Croft	21	A2
South Avenue (Castleford)	1	B2
South Avenue (Horbury)	23	C1
South Avenue (Pontefract)	19	C1
South Avenue (South Elmsall)	41	B3
South Baileygate	10	B3
South Crescent	41	C2
South Drive	25	B1
South Lane (Netherton)	31	B1
South Lane (Ossett)	23	A3
South Parade (Osset)	13	C2/C3
South Parade (Wakefield)	15	B2
South Parade	T/C	D3
South Park Way	4	C2
South Street (Havercroft)	35	C2
South Street (Hemsworth)	37	A3
South Street (Normanton)	17	A1
South Street (Ossett)	13	B3
South Street (Wakefield)	15	C2
South Street	T/C	E3
South Terrace	13	B3
South View (Castleford)	2	A3
South View (Featherstone)	19	A1
South View (Pontefract)	10	B3
South View Gardens	10	C3
Southdale Gardens	13	B2
Southdale Road	13	B2
Southfield Avenue	18	B2
Southfield Close (Horbury)	23	C1
Southfield Close (Wrenthorpe)	4	C3
Southfield Fold	23	C1
Southfield Lane	23	C1
Southfield Road (Knottingley)	11	C2
Southfield Road (Sharlston)	17	B3
Southfields View	23	A3
Southgate (Pontefract)	10	A3
Southgate (South Hiendley)	36	A3
Southgate (Wakefield)	15	B2
Southgate	T/C	D2
Southgate Close	38	A1
Southmoor Lane	12	B2
Southmoor Road	37	A3
Southwell Lane	23	B1
Sovereign Gardens	7	A3
Sowgate Lane)	10	C2/11 A2
Sowood Avenue	13	B3
Sowood Gardens	13	C3
Sowood Lane	13	C3
Sowood View	13	C3
Spa Croft Road	13	C2
Spa Grove	14	C3
Spa Lane	13	C3/14 A3
Spa Street	14	A2
Sparable Lane	15	C3
Spawd Bone Lane	11	C2
Speak Close	6	A3
Speedwell Drive	1	A3
Spink Lane	10	A3
Spinney, The	25	B2
Spital Hardwick Road	3	A3
Spitalgap Lane	20	C1/21 A1
Spout Fold	14	B1
Spring End Road	14	A3
Spring Gardens	10	A3
Spring House	40	C2
Spring Lane	27	A2
Spring Lea	40	C2
Spring Mill Lane	13	C2
Spring Terrace	41	B2
Spring Vale Road	41	A2
Spring View	13	C2
Springfield Avenue (Pontefract)	10	B3
Springfield Avenue (Hemsworth)	37	A3
Springfield Grange	14	B1
Springfield Mount	41	A3
Springfields Avenue	12	A2
Springfields	12	A2
Springhill Avenue	26	C1
Springhill Close	5	A1
Springhill Drive	26	C1
Springhill Grove	26	C1
Springhill Mount	26	C1
Springhill	26	C1
Springhills	5	A1
Springs, The	15	B1
Springs, The	T/C	D2
Springstone Avenue (Hemsworth)	37	A3
Springstone Avenue (Ossett)	13	B2
Springvale Rise	37	A2
Springville	38	B3
Springwell Road	13	B2
Spurr Grove	25	C2
Spurrier's Avenue	11	A2
Square, The (Castleford)	3	A2
Square, The (Ferrybridge)	11	A1
Squirrels Drey	24	B2
Stablers Walk	7	B2
Stadium Way	41	C1
Stafford Street	1	C1
Stafford Terrace	14	C2
Stainburn Avenue	2	B3
Stamford Avenue	1	B2
Standbridge Close	24	C3
Standbridge Garth	24	B3
Standbridge Lane	24	C3
Standing Flat Bridge	30	B2
Standish Crescent	40	C2
Stanfield Road	2	C1
Stanley Cottages	7	B3
Stanley Lane	5	B2
Stanley Road	15	C1
Stanley Road	T/C	E2
Stanley Street (Castleford)	2	A1
Stanley Street (Featherstone)	19	A1
Stanley Street (Normanton)	7	B2
Stanley Street	15	C1
Stanley Street	T/C	E2
Stanmoor Drive	5	C1
Stannard Well Drive	14	A3
Stannard Well Lane	14 A3/23 C1	
Stansfield Close	2	C1
Stansfield Drive	2	C1
Star Yard	10	A3
Starbeck Road	5	C3
Starwort Close	20	A1
Station Cottages	27	B3
Station Lane (Featherstone)	18	C2
Station Lane (Pontefract)	10	A3
Station Passage	T/C	E3
Station Road (Ackworth)	29	A2
Station Road (Castleford)	2	A1
Station Road (Ferrybridge)	11	A1
Station Road (Hemsworth)	37	A2
Station Road (Normanton)	7	A2
Station Road (Ossett)	13	B2
Station Road (Ryhill)	35	B2
Station Road (South Elmsall)	41	C2
Station Street	15	C3
Stella Gardens	10	B2
Stennard Island	15	C2
Stephenson Way	4	C2
Stevenson Avenue	3	A3
Stillwell Drive	25	B1
Stilwell Garth	25	B1
Stilwell Grove	25	B1
Stithy Street	13	A1
Stocking Lane	12	B1
Stockingate	40	C2
Stocksmoor Lane	31	B2
Stocksmoor Road	31	A1
Stone Court	36	A3
Stonecliffe Drive	22	B2
Stonecroft	5	C1
Stonegate Drive	19	C2
Stonegate Lane	28	C3
Stonegate	13	C3
Stonelea Grove	41	C3
Stoneleigh Grove	13	B2
Stoney Brook Close	31	C3
Stoney Lane (Carrgate)	4	B2
Stoney Lane (Chapelthorpe)	32	C1
Stony Hill	10	A3
Stopford Avenue	25	B2
Stopford Garth	25	B1
Storie Crescent	14	C3
Storrs Hill Road	13 B3/23 A1	
Strands Court	23	A2
Stranglands Lane	3	B2/C3
Stratheden Road	15	A1
Stratheden Road	T/C	A1
Strathmore Gardens	41	C2
Street Furlong Lane	20	C1
Stretton Close	8	B3
Strickland Road	39	A2
Stringer Lane	23	C1
Stringers Yard	23	B1
Stuart Grove	7	A2
Stuart Road	10	A3
Stuart Street (Castleford)	2	A1
Stuart Street (Pontefract)	10	A3
Stubbs Lane	21	C1
Stubley Street	T/C	C2
Stumpcross Close	10	C2
Stumpcross Court	10	C2
Stumpcross Lane	10	C2
Stumpcross Way	10	C2
Sudforth Lane	12	C2
Suffolk Close	13	A2
Sugar Lane	15	C3
Sullivan Grove	40	C3
Summer Lane	34	B3
Summer Meadow	20	A1
Sun Court	8	C3
Sun Lane	15	B1
Sun Lane	T/C	E2
Sunny Avenue (South Elmsall)	41	C2
Sunny Avenue (Upton)	38	B3
Sunny Bank (Fitzwilliam)	36	B1
Sunny Bank (Knottingley)	11	C1
Sunny Bank (Normanton)	17	B1
Sunny Bank (Ryhill)	35	B2
Sunny Bank (Upton)	38	C2
Sunny Hill Close	4	C3
Sunny Hill Croft	4	B3
Sunnybank Street	13	A2
Sunnydale Croft	13	B2
Sunnydale Park	13	B2
Sunnydale Road	13	C2
Sunnydale Terrace	13	B2
Sunnyfield Drive	36	B1
Sunnyhill Crescent	4	B3
Sunnyvale Mount	41	A2
Sunroyd Avenue	23	C1
Sunroyd Hill	23	C1
Sussex Close	37	A2
Sussex Crescent	3	A2
Suzanne Crescent	41	A2
Swale Drive	2	C1
Swales Yard	10	A3
Swallow Garth	25	A3
Swanhill Lane	20	A1
Swift Way	25	A3
Swincroft	13	B2
Swine Lane	27	B3
Swiss Street	2	A1
Swithenbank Avenue	13	A1
Swithenbank Street	13	A1
Sycamore Avenue (Alverthorpe)	14	C1
Sycamore Avenue (Knottingley)	11	B2
Sycamore Avenue (Wrenthorpe)	4	C2
Sycamore Close	11	B2
Sycamore Copse	14	C2
Sycamore Court (Bretton)	31	C2
Sycamore Court (Crofton)	26	C1
Sycamore Green	10	B3
Sycamore Grove (Alverthorpe)	14	C1
Sycamore Grove (Woodhouse)	17	B1
Sycamore Lane	31	C2
Sycamore Road	36	C3
Sycamore Street	15	C3
Sycamore Way	19	A1
Sycamores, The	23	C1
Sykes Close	28	B3
Sylvester Avenue	17	A1
Symons Street	15	B2

T

Street	Page	Grid
Tadman Street	15	B2
Talbot & Falcon Yard	15	B1
Talbot & Falcon Yard	T/C	D2
Talbot Street	7	B3
Tall Trees Drive	19	A1
Tammy Hall Street	T/C	C2
Tan House Lane	29	B2
Tanners Row	10	B3
Tanshelf Drive	10 A3/20 A1	
Tanyard Fold	33	A1
Tarn Close	3	A1
Tarn Court	5	B2
Tarn Road	19	A2
Tateley Close	13	A1
Tateley Lane	13	A1
Tatton Street	16	A3
Tavern Street	15	C2
Tavern Street	T/C	E3
Tavistock Way	24	B3
Tavora Street	15	B1
Tavora Street	T/C	D1
Taylor Close	13	C3
Taylor Crescent	13	C3
Taylor Drive	13	C3
Taylor Wood Cottages	28	A2
Teal Close	2	A3
Teall Court	13	C2
Teall Street (Osset)	13	C2
Teall Street (Wakefield)	T/C	D2
Tealls Yard	13	B2
Tees Close	2	C1
Teesdale Place	11	B2
Telford Close	1	C2
Telford Mews	1	C2
Telford Way	4	C1
Tempest Road	40	C2
Templar Street	16	A3
Temple Gardens	7	A2
Temple Place	7	A2
Temple Street	1	C2
Ten Lands Lane	35	A2
Tennyson Avenue	5	C1
Tennyson Close	3	C3
Tennyson Way	10	A2
Tenterfield Road	13	B2
Tenters Close	11	A1
Tew Street	15	B2
Thackeray Walk	3	C3
Thackray Lane	10	A3
Third Avenue (Outwood)	5	B2
Third Avenue (Upton)	38	B3
Thirlmere Drive	3	A2
Thirlmere Place	11	B3
Thirlmere Road	14	C1
Thistlewood Road	5	C2
Thomas Street (Castleford)	2	A1
Thomas Street (Hemsworth)	37	A3
Thomas Way	41	C1
Thompson Avenue	3	A2
Thompson Drive	4	C2
Thompson Street	7	B3
Thompson's Yard	15	B1
Thompson's Yard	T/C	C2
Thornbury Park	14	C3
Thornbury Road	14	C3
Thorne Close	7	C3
Thornes Lane Wharf	15	B3
Thornes Lane	15	B2
Thornes Moor Avenue	15	A3

Street	Page	Grid
Thornes Moor Close	15	A3
Thornes Moor Drive	15	A3
Thornes Moor Road	15	A3
Thornes Office Park	15	A3
Thornes Road	14 C3/15	A3
Thornhill Close (Walton)	25	C2
Thornhill Close (Middlestown)	22	B2
Thornhill Croft	25	C2
Thornhill Drive	25	C2
Thornhill Road (Castleford)	2	A2
Thornhill Road (Middlestown)	22	B1
Thornhill Street	15	B2
Thornhill Street	T/C	D3
Thornleigh Avenue	15	B3
Thornleigh Crescent	15	B3
Thornleigh Croft	15	B3
Thornleigh Drive	15	B3
Thornleigh Garth	15	B3
Thornleigh Grove	15	B3
Thornleigh Road	15	B3
Thornton Close	37	A3
Thorntree Avenue	26	B1
Thorntree Close	21	A2
Thorntree Court	26	B1
Thorpe Common Bridge	30	B3
Thorpe Gate Estate	38	B1
Thorpe Lane (Badsworth)	38	A1
Thorpe Lane (Thorpe Audlin)	30	B3
Thorpe View (Ossett)	13	B1
Thorpe View (Wakefield)	14	C2
Throstle Crest	8	B3
Throstle Row	11	B3
Tithe Barn Road	11	C1
Tithe Barn Street	23	B1
Tinsworth Road	24	B3
Tintagel Court	7	B2
Toll Bar Lane	4	B3
Toll Bar Road	1	B2
Tolson Street	13	A1
Tom Dando Close	8	A3
Tom Wood Ash Lane	39	A3
Tombridge Crescent	36	B1
Tootal Street	15	C2
Top Lane	31	B2
Top Orchard	35	B2
Top Street	36	C2
Tower Avenue	38	C2
Towers Close	26	C1
Towers Lane	27	A1
Towers Paddock	2	B2
Towlerton Lane	4	C3
Town End Avenue	29	B2
Town End	13	B2
Town Street	36	C2
Townfold	13	B2
Towngate	13	B2
Townley Road	14	B2
Towton Drive	1	B3
Trent Avenue	7	B2
Trevor Terrace	4	C1
Trigot Court	40	C2
Trilby Street	15	B1
Trilby Street	T/C	E1
Trinity Church Gate	15	B2
Trinity Church Gate	T/C	D3
Trinity Court	41	C2
Trinity Street (Pontefract)	10	A3
Trinity Street (Wakefield)	15 C3/16	A3
Trinity View	13	B1
Trinity Walk	41	C1
Troon Way	15	A3
Trough Well Lane	4	C2
Trueman Way	41	B1
Trundles Lane	12	A1
Truro Drive	7	B2
Truro Walk	7	B2
Tudor Close	20	A2
Tudor Lawns	4	C1
Tudor Way	2	C1
Tumbling Close	13	B2
Tumbling Hill	20	C2
Tun Lane	35	C3
Tup Lane	35	C2
Turn O' The Nook	13	A2
Turton Street	15	B1
Turton Street	T/C	E2
Turver's Lane	12	C2
Twain Crescent	3	A3
Twitch Hill	23	C1
Twivey Street	1	C2
Tyler Close	8	A2
Tyndale Avenue	14	B3
Tyrrell Court	14	B1

U

Street	Page	Grid
Ullswater Close	11	B3
Union Square	15	B2
Union Square	T/C	D3
Union Street (Castleford)	1	C2
Union Street (Hemsworth)	37	A3
Union Street (Ossett)	13	B2
Union Street (Wakefield)	15	B1
Union Street	T/C	D2
University Street	2	A2
Uplands, The	20	A1
Upper Hatfield Place	35	C1
Upper Lane	22 C3/31	A1
Upper Warrengate	15	B1
Upper Warrengate	T/C	E2
Upper York Street	15	B1
Upper York Street	T/C	C1
Upper Ash Grove	41	C2

V

Street	Page	Grid
Vale Avenue	11	A1
Vale Crescent	11	A1
Vale Crest	11	A1
Vale Head Grove	11	B1
Vale Head Mount	11	A1
Vale Road	36	C2
Vale View	29	B2
Valestone Avenue	37	A3
Valley Avenue	41	C2
Valley Crescent	4	C3
Valley Drive	4	C3
Valley Road (Darrington)	21	B2
Valley Road (Ossett)	13	B3
Valley Road (Pontefract)	10	A3
Valley Street	41	B2
Valley View	41	C2
Valley View Road	13	B3
Ventnor Close	13	B2
Ventnor Drive	13	B2
Ventnor Way	13	B2
Verner Street	18	C3
Vernon Place	15	B3
Vicar Lane (Horbury)	23	B1
Vicar Lane (Ossett)	13	B3
Vicarage Close (Outwood)	5	B2
Vicarage Close (South Kirkby)	40	C2
Vicarage Gardens	9	A3
Vicarage Lane	19	A2
Vicarage Mews	33	A3
Vicarage Street	T/C	D2
Vicarage Street North	15	B1
Vicarage Street North	T/C	D1
Vicarage Street	15	B1
Vickers Avenue	41	A3
Vickers Street	2	A2
Victor Road	40	C2
Victor Street (Castleford)	1	C3
Victor Street (South Elmsall)	41	B2
Victoria Avenue	15	A1
Victoria Avenue	T/C	A2
Victoria Court (Castleford)	1	C2
Victoria Court (Horbury)	23	B1
Victoria Court (Upton)	38	B3
Victoria Grove	14	B3
Victoria Place	2	A1
Victoria Street (Ackworth)	28	B3
Victoria Street (Castleford)	1	C2
Victoria Street (Featherstone)	18 C2/19	A2
Victoria Street (Hemsworth)	37	A2
Victoria Street (Horbury)	23	B1
Victoria Street (Outwood)	5	A2
Victoria Street (Pontefract)	10	A2
Victoria Street (Wakefield)	15	A1
Victoria Street	T/C	A1
Victoria Approach	5	A2
Victoria Way	5	A2
Victory Lane	6	A3
Viking Road	10	B3
Villa Close	29	B2
Villas, The	27	C2
Virginia Close	5	A1
Virginia Court	5	A1
Virginia Drive	5	A1
Virginia Gardens	5	A1
Vissett Close	36	C3
Vissitt Lane	36	B3

W

Street	Page	Grid
Wadhouse Lane	24	B1
Waggon Lane	38	C3
Waindike Close	7	C2
Waindike Way	7	C3
Waite Street	14	C1
Wakefield Road (Ackworth)	28	C3
Wakefield Road (Bretton)	31	A3
Wakefield Road (Featherstone)	18	B2
Wakefield Road (Horbury)	14 B3/23	C1
Wakefield Road (Kinsley)	36	B1
Wakefield Road (Lupset)	14	A2
Wakefield Road (Normanton)	7 B3/17	A1
Wakefield Road (Ossett)	13	C1
Wakefield Road (Pontefract)	19	C1
Wakefield Road (Streethouse)	17	C2
Walden Street	2	A2
Waldenhowe Close	8	C3
Waldorf Way	15	B2
Walker Avenue	14	C1
Walker Lane	23	C1
Walkergate	10	B3
Wallace Gardens	5	A1
Walled Garden, The	33	A3
Walmsley Drive	38	C3
Walnut Avenue	14	C1
Walnut Close	19	C2
Walnut Crescent	14	C1
Walnut Drive (Normanton)	17	B1
Walnut Drive (Pontefract)	19	C2
Walnut Street	41	B3
Walton Lane	25	B1
Walton Road	39	A2
Walton Station Lane	25	B2
Walton View	26	C1
Ward Lane	6	A2
Warmfield Lane	16	C1
Warmfield View	15	C1
Warneford Avenue	13	B1
Warren Avenue (Knottingley)	11	A2
Warren Avenue (Wakefield)	15	B3
Warren Court	T/C	E2
Warren Drive	8	B3
Warwick Street	16	A3
Wasdale Crescent	14	C1
Wasdale Road	14	C1
Watchit Hole Lane	30	B3
Water Lane (East Hardwick)	20	A3
Water Lane (Hemsworth)	40	B1
Water Lane (Middlestown)	23	A1
Water Lane (Pontefract)	10	B2
Water Lane (Stanley)	6	A2
Water Lane (Woolley)	33	A3
Water Lane Close	23	A2
Watergate	10	A3
Waterhouse Grove	15	A1
Waterhouse Grove	T/C	A2
Waterloo Close	1	A3
Waterloo Street	15	B2
Waterton Close (South Kirkby)	41	A2
Waterton Close (Walton)	25	C2
Waterton Grove	14	C2
Waterton Road	14	C2
Waterton Street	1	C2
Watling Road	3	A1
Watson Crescent	15	C1
Watson Crescent	T/C	F1
Watson Street	7	B3
Watsons Yard	23	B1
Wauchope Street	15	B2
Waulkmill Close	38	B3
Wavell Garth	25	B2
Wavell Grove	25	B2
Weavers Road	10	B3
Webster Place	7	B3
Weeland Avenue	17	B3
Weeland Court	11	C1
Weeland Crescent	17	C3
Weeland Drive	17	C3
Weeland Road (Crofton)	17	B3
Weeland Road (Knottingley)	11	C1
Weetworth Avenue	2	A2
Weetworth Park	2	A2
Welbeck Lane	6	A3
Welbeck Street (Castleford)	1	C2
Welbeck Street (Wakefield)	15	C3
Welburn Close	25	B1
Wellesley Green	14	C1
Wellgarth Road	19	A3
Wellgate (Castleford)	2	B2
Wellgate (Ossett)	13	B2
Wellhead Mews	24	B3
Wellington Place	11	B1
Wellington Street (Alverthorpe)	14	C1
Wellington Street (Castleford)	1	C2
Wells Court	13	A2
Wensley Drive	20	B1
Wensley Street	23	B1
Wensley Street East	23	B1
Went Avenue	18	C3
Went Bridge	30	C2
Went Croft	20	A2
Went Edge Road	30	C2
Went Fold	20	A2
Went Garth	20	A2
Went Grove	18	C3
Went Hill Close	29	A1
Went Lane	28	B2
Went View	30	B3
Wentbridge Road	19	A2
Wentcliffe Road	11	A1
Wentdale Road	20	A2
Wentwell Road	17	C2
Wentworth Close	32	C3
Wentworth Drive (Crofton)	26	C1
Wentworth Drive (South Kirkby)	40	C2
Wentworth Park Rise	21	A2
Wentworth Road	18	C2
Wentworth Street	15	A1
Wentworth Street	T/C	C1
Wentworth Terrace (Fitzwilliam)	36	B1
Wentworth Terrace (Wakefield)	T/C	C1
Wentworth Way	25	B1
Wesley Court	13	A2
Wesley Hall Court	6	A3
Wesley Place	19	A2
Wesley Street (Castleford)	2	A1
Wesley Street (Cutsyke)	1	C3
Wesley Street (Ossett)	13	A2
Wesley Street (South Elmsall)	41	A2
Wesley Street (Wakefield)	15	C3
West Avenue (Horbury)	23	C1
West Avenue (Pontefract)	19	C1
West Avenue (South Elmsall)	41	C1
West Avenue (Upton)	38	B3
West Close (Carleton)	20	B2
West Close (Normanton)	7	A2
West Drive	20	B1
West End Avenue	8	B3
West Ings Close	12	A1
West Ings Court	12	A1
West Ings Crescent	12	A1
West Ings Lane	12	A1
West Ings Mews	12	A1
West Ings Way	12	A1
West Lane	17 B3/27	A1
West Mead	2	B2
West Moor Road	36	B1
West Parade	15	B2
West Parade	T/C	D3
West Parade Court	15	B2
West Parade Court	T/C	D3
West Parade Street	15	B2
West Parade Street	T/C	D3
West Park Drive	21	B3
West Park Terrace	21	A3
West Street (Castleford)	1	C1
West Street (Havercroft)	35	C2
West Street (Hemsworth)	36	C2

Street	Map	Grid
West Street (Lupset)	15	A2
West Street (Normanton)	7	B3
West Street (South Elmsall)	41	C2
West Street (South Hiendley)	36	A3
West Street (South Kirkby)	40	A3
West Street (Stanley)	6	A3
West View (Ackworth)	28	B3
West View (Altofts)	7	A2
West View (Horse Race End)	16	B3
West View (Kirkhamgate)	4	A3
West View (Knottingley)	12	A2
West View (Ossett)	13	A2
West View (Painthorpe)	24	A3
West View Avenue	2	B2
West View Terrace	14	B1
West Wells Crescent	13	A2
West Wells Road	13	A2
Westbourne Avenue	19	C1
Westbourne Close	25	A2
Westbourne Crescent	19	C1
Westbourne Drive	19	C1
Westbourne Mount	19	C1
Westcroft Drive	13	A1
Westcroft Road	36	C2
Westerman Close	19	A1/A2
Westerman Street	15	C3
Western Avenue	10	B3
Western Court	10	B3
Westfield Avenue (Castleford)	1	C3
Westfield Avenue (Knottingley)	11	C2
Westfield Avenue (Pontefract)	20	A1
Westfield Buildings	41	B2
Westfield Bungalows	41	B2
Westfield Close	7	A3
Westfield Court	13	C3
Westfield Crescent (Ossett)	13	A2
Westfield Crescent (Kirkhamgate)	4	A2
Westfield Crescent (Ryhill)	35	A2
Westfield Drive	13	A2
Westfield Farm	13	A2
Westfield Grove (Ackworth)	29	B2
Westfield Grove (Castleford)	1	C3
Westfield Grove Wakefield)	5	B3
Westfield Lane (Darrington)	21	A2/30 C1
Westfield Lane (South Elmsall)	41	B2
Westfield Park	5	B3
Westfield Place	4	A2
Westfield Road (Horbury)	23	B1
Westfield Road (Knottingley)	11	C2
Westfield Road (Hemsworth)	36	C2
Westfield Road	15	B1
Westfield Street	13	A2
Westfield Terrace (Horbury)	23	B1
Westfield Terrace (Pontefract)	9	C3
Westfield Terrace (Wakefield)	15	B1
Westfield View	5	B3
Westfield	13	A2
Westfields	1	C3
Westgate (Hemsworth)	36	C3
Westgate (Wakefield)	15	B1
Westgate	T/C	C2
Westgate End	15	A2
Westgate End	T/C	A3
Westlea Cottages	11	C2
Westmorland Street	T/C	D2
Westmount Street	9	C3
Westoff Lane	35	C2
Westways Close	4	C2
Westways Rise	4	C3
Westways	4	C2
Westwood Close	19	A1
Westwood Road (Ossett)	13	C2
Westwood Road (Castleford)	1	C3
Westwood Street	13	C2
Wharfe Way	2	C1
Wharfedale Drive	7	B2
Wharncliffe Road	24	C3
Wheatcroft	2	C2
Wheatings, The	13	C2
Wheatley Avenue	7	B3
Wheatroyd Crescent	13	A3
Wheldon Road	2	B1
Whin Close	37	A3
Whin Mount	7	C3
Whincop Avenue	1	B2
Whinfield Place	14	A3
Whinney Moor Avenue	14	C3
Whinny Close	17	C2
Whinny Lane	17	C2
Whisperwood Close	5	C1
Whisperwood Road	5	C1
White Cross Gardens	35	C3
White Horse Yard	15	B1
White Horse Yard	T/C	C2
White House Bungalows	15	A3
White's Buildings	13	B1
White's Road	T/C	D2
White Apron Street	40	C2
Whitebeam Green	10	B3
Whitegate Hill	29	C1
Whitegate Lane	29	C1/C2
Whitegates Close	5	A3
Whitehall Avenue	5	A3
Whitehall Court	23	B1
Whitehall Crescent	5	A3
Whitehall Rise	5	A3
Whitehall Street	14	C2
Whiteley Street	19	A2
Whites Row	23	A1
Whitley Spring Crescent	13	C2
Whitley Spring Road	13	C2
Whitley Street	19	A2
Whitwood Common Lane	1	A3
Whitwood Lane	1	A3
Whitwood Terrace	1	A3
Wicken Tree Lane	22	C2
Wickets, The	25	B1
Wild's Yard	15	B2
Wild's Yard	T/C	D3
William Prince Grove	15	C2
William Street	15	B2
William Street	T/C	E3
Willow Beck	34	A3
Willow Bridge	1	A3
Willow Court (Castleford)	2	A2
Willow Court (Featherstone)	8	C3
Willow Court (Flanshaw)	14	B1
Willow Crescent	7	B3
Willow Drive (Hemsworth)	36	C3
Willow Drive (Wakefield)	15	C3
Willow Gardens (Flanshaw)	14	B1
Willow Gardens (Townville)	3	A3
Willow Garth (Durkar)	24	B2
Willow Garth (Featherstone)	8	C3
Willow Garth (South Elmsall)	41	C2
Willow Grange	36	C2
Willow Green	5	A2
Willow Grove (Ossett)	13	B3
Willow Grove (Wakefield)	15	C3
Willow Lane (Featherstone)	8	C3
Willow Lane (Flanshaw)	14	B1
Willow Lane (Kirkthorpe)	16	C1
Willow Lane East	8	C3
Willow Mews	14	B1
Willow Mount	14	B1
Willow Park (Outwood)	5	A2
Willow Park (Pontefract)	10	B3
Willow Road (Castleford)	2	A2
Willow Road (Flanshaw)	14	B1
Willow Road (Knottingley)	11	C1
Willow View	14	B1
Willowbridge Lane	1	B2
Willowdene Lane	10	A2
Willows, The (Crigglestone)	24	B3
Willows, The (Horbury)	23	B1
Wilman Drive	13	A2
Wilman Post	13	A2
Wilson Avenue	14	A2
Wilson Court	5	B2
Wilson Drive	5	B2
Wilson Street (Castleford)	1	C2
Wilson Street (Featherstone)	18	C2
Wilson Street (Pontefract)	10	A3
Wilson Terrace	15	B2
Winchester Close	4	B3
Winchester Way	41	C1
Winden Close (Crigglestone)	24	A2
Winden Close (Outwood)	5	B1
Winden Grove	5	B1
Windermere Drive	11	B3
Windermere Road (Alverthorpe)	14	C1
Windermere Road (Castleford)	3	A2
Windhill Crescent	15	C1
Windhill Road	15	C1/16 A1
Windhill View	15	C1
Windross Close	7	A2
Windsor Avenue	29	B2
Windsor Crescent	5	A3
Windsor Drive	11	A1
Windsor Rise	19	C2
Windsor Road (Hemsworth)	37	B3
Windsor Road (Wrenthorpe)	4	C3
Windsor Street	41	C2
Windyridge Street	23	1b
Wingate Croft	25	B1
Wingate Grove	25	B1
Wintersett Lane	26	C3
Witmore Street	41	C2
Witton Street	15	B1
Witton Street	T/C	D1
Wolsey Avenue	19	C1
Womersley Road	11	C2
Wonder Street	15	B2
Wonder Street	T/C	D3
Wood Close (Altofts)	7	A2
Wood Close (Kinsley)	36	B1
Wood Green	1	B3
Wood Grove	13	B1
Wood Lane (Castleford)	1	B3
Wood Lane (Chapelthorpe)	33	A1
Wood Lane (Middlestown)	22	A2
Wood Moor Road	37	A2
Wood Mount	22	A2
Wood Street (Castleford)	1	C2
Wood Street (Ossett)	13	B1
Wood Street (Sharlston)	17	B3
Wood Street (South Hiendley)	36	A3
Wood Street (Wakefield)	15	B1
Wood Street	T/C	C2
Wood View Avenue	1	B2
Wood View Close	1	B2
Wood View Crescent	1	B2
Wood View	1	B2
Wood Yard Cottages	25	C1
Woodalls	11	C1
Woodbine Avenue	10	A3
Woodbine Street	13	B1
Woodbridge Close	15	C1
Woodbridge Close	T/C	F2
Woodcock Street	15	C3
Woodcock Way	41	C1
Woodcroft	25	B1
Woodfield Park	25	C2
Woodhall Close (Middletown)	22	A2
Woodhall Close (Durkar)	24	B2
Woodhall Drive	28	C3
Woodhouse Crescent	7	B3
Woodhouse Lane (Woolley)	33	A3
Woodhouse Mount	7	A3
Woodhouse Road	15	C1
Woodhouse Road	T/C	F2
Woodland Avenue	16	B1
Woodland Close	32	C1
Woodland Drive	25	A2
Woodland Grove	29	A1
Woodland Rise	14	B2
Woodland Road	14	B2
Woodland View (Pontefract)	20	B1
Woodland View (Sharlston)	16	C3
Woodland Way	39	A2
Woodlands (Crofton)	26	B1
Woodlands (Horbury)	23	C1
Woodlands (Ossett)	13	B1
Woodlands Avenue	2	C2
Woodlands Crescent	37	A2
Woodlands, The	20	B1
Woodlea	41	B2
Woodleigh Crescent	28	B3
Woodmoor Close	24	A3
Woodmoor Drive	24	A3
Woodmoor Rise	24	A3
Woodmoor Road (Hemsworth)	37	A2
Woodmoor Road (Kettlethorpe)	24	C3
Woodside (Castleford)	3	A1
Woodside (Wrenthorpe)	4	C2
Woodside Avenue (Sharlston)	17	B3
Woodside Avenue (Wrenthorpe)	4	C2
Woodside Crescent	17	B3
Woodside Drive	4	C3
Woodthorpe Close	25	B2
Woodthorpe Drive	25	B2
Woodthorpe Gardens	25	A2
Woodthorpe Glades	25	A2
Woodthorpe Lane	25	A2
Woodthorpe Park Drive	25	B2
Woodville Court	25	A1
Wool Market	10	A3
Woolford Way	5	C1
Woolgreaves Avenue	25	A2
Woolgreaves Close	25	A2
Woolgreaves Croft	25	A3
Woolgreaves Drive	25	A2
Woolgreaves Garth	25	A2
Woolley Edge Lane	32	B3
Woolley Edge	32	B3
Woolley Low Moor Lane	32	B1
Woolley Mill Lane	33	C3
Woolley Park Gardens	33	A3
Woolley View	32	C1
Woolpack's Yard	15	B1
Woolpacks Yard	T/C	C2
Wordsworth Drive	3	C3
Wordsworth Grove	5	C1
Wordsworth Yard	10	A3
Wordsworth Approach	10	A2
Worrall Road	24	B3
Wortley Place	36	C3
Wrangbrook Lane	39	A3
Wrangbrook Road	39	A2
Wrays Buildings	23	B1
Wren Croft	10	A2
Wren Garth	25	A3
Wrenthorpe Lane	4	B3
Wrenthorpe Road	4	C2
Wycliffe Street	13	A1
Wynford Drive	41	B2
Wynthorpe Road	23	C1

Y

Street	Map	Grid
Yew Tree Street	15	C3
Yew Tree Walk	11	B2
York Close	41	C1
York Place	29	B2
York Street (Altofts)	7	A2
York Street (Castleford)	2	A1
York Street (Hemsworth)	37	A3
York Street (Wakefield)	15	B1
York Villas	7	B3

Z

Street	Map	Grid
Zetland Street	15	B1
Zetland Street	T/C	D2
Zion Street	13	A1

Wakefield Metropolitan District Council takes great care to ensure the information in this publication is accurate.
If you do find any mistakes or ommisions, please let us know by telephoning 01924 305290 or writing to:
Head of Administration, Ref. Official Map, Wakefield MDC, County Hall, Bond Street, WAKEFIELD WF1 2QW